Sue *signature*

D1415104

SPEAKING TO SILENCE

New Rites for Christian Worship and Healing

JANET S. PETERMAN

Westminster John Knox Press
LOUISVILLE • LONDON

© 2007 Janet S. Peterman

All rights reserved. Except where noted in the acknowledgments, no part of this book may be reproduced or transmitted in any form or by any means, electronic or mechanical, including photocopying, recording, or by any information storage or retrieval system, without permission in writing from the publisher. For information, address Westminster John Knox Press, 100 Witherspoon Street, Louisville, Kentucky 40202-1396.

Scripture quotations, unless otherwise indicated, are from the New Revised Standard Version of the Bible, copyright © 1989 by the Division of Christian Education of the National Council of the Churches of Christ in the U.S.A., and used by permission.

See Acknowledgments, pp. 188–90, for additional permission information and reprint information for local ministry settings.

Book design by Teri Kay Vinson
Cover design by Pam Poll Graphic Design
Cover art: El Kuriki/Getty Images

First edition
Published by Westminster John Knox Press
Louisville, Kentucky

This book is printed on acid-free paper that meets the American National Standards Institute Z39.48 standard. ∞

PRINTED IN THE UNITED STATES OF AMERICA

07 08 09 10 11 12 13 14 15 16 — 10 9 8 7 6 5 4 3 2 1

Library of Congress Cataloging-in-Publication Data is on file at the Library of Congress, Washington, D.C.

ISBN-13: 978-0-664-22880-4
ISBN-10: 0-664-22880-1

*For Kent
and for our children,
Phoebe, Neil, and Nathaniel*

*I thank my God every time I remember you.
(Phil. 1:3)*

Contents

Preface

You will not see it written directly in these pages, but I have been nurtured in two faith traditions. Raised in the Lutheran Church and called forth into leadership there as a teen, it was also there that I first heard a call to ministry. I am deeply rooted in the movement of the liturgical seasons, in the changing color of paraments and the biblical texts of the lectionary, in the rhythm of Word and Sacrament each Sunday, with the strains of organ, choir, and hymns sung in four-part harmony. Though my family was in church every week for as long as I can remember, Christmas Eve in my grandparents' church when I was perhaps ten or twelve is one of my earliest memories of belonging to the Church. Mount Calvary's members were Lutherans of German descent, my grandmother belonging to the first generation born here. Deep in the night, all dark but for the small candles in our hands, surrounded by family, we sang "Silent Night," then listened to the story of Jesus' birth from Luke 2. In the radiance of that candlelight, I knew the wonder and mystery of the incarnation, the Word of God made flesh and living among us: "*to you* is born this day . . . a Savior . . ." (Luke 2:11; emphasis added).

For twenty-five years I have served as a pastor in urban Lutheran churches, living and working in communities more African American than White, surrounded by Christian brothers and sisters in Baptist and Pentecostal churches whom Lutherans rarely consider ecumenical partners. Yet it was there within the various worship traditions and ministries of the Black Church that I discovered a part of myself I couldn't have named earlier as missing. There I could move to the oral rhythms of preaching and praise gospel music, could weep with the spirituals, could find myself within the biblical Exodus story— looking to God who makes a way out of no way. There I could learn to celebrate the resurrection of Jesus Christ, could understand community in both physical and spiritual terms, and could find my own voice for praise of God, even while serving in the midst of poverty and despair.

In myriad ways both simple and profound, *Speaking to Silence* arises out of this double blessing, of a faith experience in two cultures, and of the theological experiences of both incarnation and resurrection. Like the psalmist, I give thanks to God for the deepening of faith on my spiritual journey:

> Thou, LORD, my allotted portion,
>   thou my cup, thou dost enlarge my boundaries.
>   Ps. 16:5–6, *New English Bible*

Many have called forth my gifts of leadership and have offered their support to me through the course of this writing. While a divinity school student, worship and music came alive for me in a new way as I worshiped with Pastor Henry E. Horn at University Lutheran Church in Cambridge. Gordon Lathrop, Charles A. Schieren Professor Emeritus of Liturgy at the Lutheran Theological Seminary in Philadelphia, helped me to shape a sabbatical project that became the kernel of this book. Elaine J. Ramshaw, author of a seminal book on the relationship between worship and pastoral care, tutored me in ways that psychologists use ritual and provided engaging conversation. Dorothy Bass's and Sheryl Fullerton's interest and early suggestions gave me hope that I might one day publish my work. As developmental editor, Naomi Lucks of YouCanWrite.com helped me cut through piles of paper to find the heart of my work.

Pastor Mary Forell called on me to write a liturgy for her when she faced surgery, showing me that my earlier work with miscarriage and stillbirth was the first part of a new direction in my ministry, rather than an isolated writing project. Her thoughtful readings of the manuscript at various stages always added strength to my work. Mary and I are part of a long-running retreat group with Pastors Gladys Moore and Barbara Lundblad, a group my daughter, when young, once named simply The Women. In their presence I have discovered both my own gifts for ministry and the courage to be myself. I have flourished in the difficult work of urban parish ministry in no small way because of our common life together.

For nearly twenty-four years, I served as a pastor of St. Michael's Lutheran Church in the Mt. Airy section of Philadelphia. I grew into my role as pastor among the people of St. Michael's Church and its surrounding community. It was most often with them, and with Pastor Violet Cucciniello Little, with whom I shared the ministry for fourteen years, that these new worship materials came to life. My heart overflows with gratitude for our life together in those years, a life that is woven into every page of this book.

Many pastors and lay leaders shared their stories with me or shared their work in creating new rituals. I could never hope to be able to name all of them from the nine years of the book's preparation. They will see themselves in these pages and I thank them. In addition to those whose work appears in the book itself, whose names you will find there, the following have also been instrumental in a variety of ways: Jann Boyd, Jessica Crist-Graybill, Harvey Davis, Talia de Lone, Valerie Elverton Dixon, Wayne Dreyman, Tom F. Driver, Jim Dunlop, Donna Skinner Echols, James Kenneth Echols, Urla Eversley, Gary George, Pam Holliman, Nicole Johnson, G. Daniel Jones, John Keating, Leroy Miles, Constance F. Parvey, Dorothy Peterman, Fred and Kathy Powell, Stephen Ray, Rodney Roberson, Cathy Rosenholtz, Alan Smith, Susan Smith, Roger Stephens, Nile Weber, and Larry Wheelock. Though I accept full responsibility for any shortcomings in the final work, I want to thank each of these friends, family members, and colleagues publicly for their support of my ministry and my writing. I thank God for them.

Within Westminster John Knox Press, Vice President Jack Keller early saw the strength of my work, and his support has brought the book to fruition—a special thanks to him. Stephanie Egnotovich's fine line-by-line editing sharpened the book's focus. Julie Tonini guided the book through production. All of them have made the book stronger, and I thank them.

This book would not have been possible without financial support that allowed me time for reflection two steps away from the daily press of ministry. With gratitude I acknowledge two grants from the Louisville Institute, including a Sabbatical Grant for Pastoral Leaders in 1997. I'm grateful for the Institute's support and for the encouragement of their Executive Director, James W. Lewis. Support for the writing of *Speaking to Silence* was provided by the Valparaiso Project on the Education and Formation of People in Faith. To the project and its director, Dorothy Bass, I offer my gratitude and thanks.

Finally, a word of gratitude for my family: my father-in-law, Pastor C. Wayne Peterman, now of blessed memory, showed me with his life that it is possible to be a faithful pastor *and* a husband and parent who is present to his home and family. His life example encouraged me early on to nurture the roots of family and of faith, a rhythm readers will recognize in these pages. My parents, Duane R. and Joanne M. Smith, consciously shape their schedule in retirement to spend time with their grandchildren, and they have also made time to assist with the extra demands of my writing. We are grateful for their presence in our lives. My husband, Kent, has read these chapters more than any other single person, offering, always, supportive ways to strengthen my use of language. More than that, he has helped me to articulate the heart of my ministry. For his love, and for our life together with our children, Phoebe, Neil, and Nathaniel, I am more grateful than words can say.

Pastor Janet S. Peterman
All Saints' Day 2006

Introduction

If the LORD had not been my help,
my soul would . . . have lived in the land of silence.
Ps. 94:17

I began this work as a Christian pastor, called out one night to a place where I had never been. When I think of that night, I remember most the silent hallway of the large city hospital, how quiet it was. It was late on a Sunday—Pentecost Sunday, at that—after a big church celebration; I was tired. But the woman's story filled my heart. "You don't know how grateful I am that you came," the nurse was saying. She was guiding me back outside after my visit, through a confusing maze as we walked away from the woman's room. The hospital had placed the woman at the end of a long corridor, with empty rooms all around her, far, it seemed, from anything else. "She was traveling far from home," the nurse continued, "when she went into labor—but too soon." The woman had been waiting alone in her room for more than three hours, unwilling to relinquish her baby's body until the baby could be baptized by a pastor.

"I know it's Sunday evening," I asked the nurse, "but why did it take you so long to find someone to come?"

"There were people who could come," she answered, "but they wouldn't. They said, 'We don't baptize dead babies.'"

Suddenly my heart seemed to stop. I wanted to rush out of that strange place and get home under cover of darkness. I heard these words reverberate inside me: We don't baptize dead babies, either!

What had I done?

If you come from a tradition that does not baptize infants, you may have a hard time grasping the crisis this woman faced that Pentecost night. A faithful church member, she had been taught that it was her Christian duty as a

xiii

mother to have her child baptized for the sake of the child's salvation. It makes little difference whether that is exactly what she had been taught, or whether the teaching was distorted now through her experience of grief. She was determined to have her child baptized before giving up the body.

In the moment of her crisis, short of not going to be with her, I could imagine no way of denying the mother's request. With sterile water and a metal bowl from hospital supplies, I baptized Diana Lynn and handed her back to God.

Over the next months, I came to ask a different question. Not what had I done, but what if . . . ? What if Christian tradition provided a recognized alternative to use in such circumstances? What if this mother knew from the worship practices of her own church that should a pregnancy ever end in loss—whether through miscarriage or stillbirth—that the Church had a word from God and that this Word included an affirmation of the uniqueness of this child or pregnancy; an acknowledgment of the parents' grief and of the death they experienced; and words of reassurance about God's love in Jesus, arms stretched wide open on the cross, arms of saving mercy wide enough to receive their child?

I began looking for such a resource, certain that I would find the material somewhere. I knew that my own Lutheran worship tradition provided a few readings and prayers, but not enough to be helpful in that hospital room, and nothing for the even more common experience of miscarriage. I spent a long time looking. Mostly, I found the same silence I had experienced in the hospital hallway.

Most traditions, I discovered, say little or nothing about parents' fears for their child's salvation. One dominant message about pregnancy loss comes from the medical field: this was a life that was not intended to be. If it was "not really a life," it could not therefore now be an experience of death. Medical personnel, family members, and friends also tended to deny the uniqueness of the pregnancy, especially for earlier losses in pregnancy. ("She's young. Let her go home and have another.") But I knew that parents of these babies and pregnancies often experienced deep grief. What role might the Church play in helping them through their difficulty?

In that silence, I began to listen and to hear. Biblical lessons and hymns began floating into my awareness while I was gardening, making my family's meals, or working on sermons for my congregation. But we have *this* to say to her, I realized, and *this*. By the urgings of the Holy Spirit I was drawn for the first time into creating a new ritual. That rite, "Remembrance and Commendation of a Stillborn Child or after a Miscarriage" (pp. 127–34), speaks to real human needs. Its readings and prayers show God to be the God of compassion who does not willfully inflict suffering and death. The ritual acknowledges the loss publicly as a death experience, even if only at the hospital or with a small group of people. It offers comfort for grief, makes space for the voices of the parents and others, as appropriate, both to shape the experience and to speak in the service. It also provides an opportunity to name the child, acknowledging the uniqueness of what was lost. Throughout, the ritual gives voice to the human need for God's mercy, as we know it in Jesus Christ.

The rite has been reprinted and reshaped literally thousands of times—in local settings, in congregations, in hospitals, and among friends. Nearly twenty years later, I still receive calls each year for copies or for counsel on how to use it.

It is not that only these particular words will do, nor that the suggested prayers, readings, songs, and public naming are the only possible ritual for such an occasion. Like good worship experiences everywhere, these words have been helpful because real people take them into their hands, shape them to fit their own circumstances, and use them to speak in a time of profound need. The rite works when someone is there to listen to the cries of a mother or a father who has just lost a child; when someone dares to call forth the presence of God, who will stand with us: It is deep speaking to deep.

In such a gathering, we cannot remain the same as we were: We are transformed; we have been heard, moved out of the experience of suffering alone, and carried to a new place. As theologian Tom Driver writes, Our "prayer[s] . . . transform isolation into community, emptiness into fullness, despair into hope."[1] For where two or three are gathered in my name, says Jesus, I am there among them (Matt. 18:20).

WALKING INTO THE SILENCE

Our ministries sometimes call us out to be with people in places where we have never been before. Many of the worship resources in this book came into being as I stood in those places in my ministry. I came to understand that ritual is uniquely capable of bringing a word from God in the context of real and sometimes desperate human needs.

In this book, I want to show pastors and other worship leaders a new way of thinking about ritual—that they might imagine worship experiences as part of the pastoral care offered by their congregations. The twenty-one rituals offered here are available to readers to use or adapt.

Many authors, poets, musicians, and religious leaders have granted permission for their materials to be used freely in this way, that the worship life of the church might thereby deepen and grow. I ask that you honor their gifts by acknowledging my work and theirs as you use them (see acknowledgments, pp. 188–90).

This book arises out of the pastoral conviction that if worship is to speak in the silence, it needs to be created from many angles, in myriad local settings. So the rituals appearing in this book serve a dual purpose: to provide new worship materials for use and adaptation, and to offer the rituals as examples of a wide range of new ritual possibilities. I hope that the appearance of these materials here will unleash the creativity of pastors and others with the gifts of leadership to take up the work themselves of creating new worship materials.

This book thus serves a kind of teaching function, which is evident in two ways. First, the book's beginning and ending, its framework, provide reflections on the character of ritual in general and of new rituals specifically, as well as a suggested process for creating new worship materials. Part 1, "Understanding Ritual," includes chapter 1, which lays the groundwork with a discussion of the nature of ritual, and chapter 2, which reflects on characteristics of ritual in new contexts. Part 3 (chapter 7), "Creating New Rituals for Christian Worship," describes a seven-step process for creating new ritual materials and offers further reflections on adapting existing worship materials for use in new settings. Readers will see the book's teaching function partly through these discursive sections.

Second, readers will discover a more subtle teaching approach by working with the rituals in chapters 3 through 6. The four chapters of part 2 provide the substantive weight of the book. A broad spectrum of rituals are included in these chapters: rituals for personal use, for life in the home or at church, or for use in the wider community; rituals used in preparation for an event like surgery or as a response to difficult circumstances; rituals that mark an event in the life cycle; and rituals that help effect transformation. Clustered together in groups of rituals around a similar theme, these chapters ("Ritual Signs of New Life and New Community"; "Making Holy What Has Been Violated"; "Rituals for Recovery"; and "Rituals of Blessing in the Presence of Death") are each introduced with reflections on the area of ministry represented.

In these introductions, readers will first find a brief discussion of the pastoral issues involved in a particular area of ministry. Using stories from pastoral ministry and community life, I name some common threads among many who experience these circumstances, suggesting issues that worship leaders will want to keep in mind as they plan and use the ritual or create their own materials. The introductions serve to sharpen the focus of readers' listening—to show how particular circumstances call forth ritual responses of one kind or direction rather than another. They are, however, suggestive. Two people facing what appears to be the same circumstance can have vastly different emotional reactions and therefore have quite different needs for a rite. Among women I have known who had a mastectomy because of cancer, for example, one felt mainly relief that doctors had found the cancer early enough and glad for the chance for reconstructive surgery; another felt mainly grief at her loss and couldn't imagine the gain of reconstructive surgery. The suggestions offered here are meant to lead you to assess what will work in your setting, with the needs you discover in your community.

Reflecting through four chapters of widely varied ritual examples will also help readers begin to apply their own discernment skills to the circumstances they face in their ministries. Questions raised in the course of such reflection will draw the reader back to the more didactic portions of the text, and specifically to the exercises for creating new rituals in chapter 7.

USING THE RITUALS IN THIS VOLUME

A few remarks will help you access the worship materials offered here.

First, each of the rituals contained in this book is offered complete, from beginning to end, including all of the prayers, with suggestions for biblical texts and music. Some readers will want to use the rituals in this form. Others come to the rituals from more-oral worship traditions, where free prayer and improvisation are essential to worship's meaning. By all means—please!—use your own approach. Adapt these rituals to fit your situation; substitute prayers from your church's worship book, or use free prayer; choose music or texts meaningful in your setting; lead the worship in a way appropriate to your local or denominational traditions, according to the spiritual practices of your community.

Throughout the book, the one leading the ritual is called simply "Leader." Most often a pastor or minister could fill that role, though often others might, too. Active laypeople who take on worship leadership in a congregation, spiritual leaders of a ministry, deacons, Sunday school teachers, spiritual friends, or prayer partners—any of these leaders might, with the right sensitivity or leadership experience in your congregation, be able to step into the leadership role for a particular ritual. There are, however, some cautions about who might best not take on that role.

In a ritual gathering of a family—say, for example, the ritual for a family with an Alzheimer's patient or the ritual return to the grave—it is especially important to choose as worship leader someone outside the family. When family members share their reflections, the leader moderates, making sure that a few do not dominate. This is a role that a family member, as a member of the group, cannot perform. Minsters or other worship leaders from a congregation would better carry that leadership.

Some participants will have trouble sharing certain deeply personal ritual experiences with their pastor. There are places in the recovery cycle of rituals in chapter 5 where this would often be true. Suggestions are offered in that chapter's introduction for ways of extending a congregation's ministry when the church's pastor will not be leading the worship experience. Similar suggestions are offered with the breast rite in chapter 6.

In the body of the rituals themselves, italicized font indicates variable portions of the text. The leader inserts the appropriate words: for example, *John* as *he* celebrates this anniversary *of sobriety*, or *Shirl* as *she* celebrates *thirteen years of clean time.*

And finally, a word about silence. Whatever the Sunday morning worship experience of your congregation, whether your worship is primarily contemplative or more emotionally filled praise, those who lead these more-occasional rituals will often need to pay closer attention to the use of silence than they do for regular Sunday morning worship. Holding silence together with others, as it is recommended during the visualization used with bereaved survivors of suicide, can be crucial to the ritual's movement: Do not rush through the silences. Leaving long-enough silences during times when participants share reflections also allows those who are slower to speak aloud enough time to come to voice. It often takes more time than leaders imagine to draw out the quietest members of a group.

PERCEIVING THE SILENCE IN OUR TRADITION

The experience both of that Pentecost baptism and of preparing new worship materials opened a new door in my ministry. I began to perceive other silences in the church's traditions. Perhaps you have also felt them.

I have felt the burden of silence while standing beside someone recovering from addiction or trying desperately to begin the process of recovery. I have longed to have the right words when working with couples who have resolved to stop infertility treatments to get on with the rest of their lives; or when they acknowledge that the marriage they've been trying so hard to save will *not* be saved. I have wanted words to help a family bless an aged parent's transition to a nursing home or to reclaim for the living a place robbed of hope by an act of violence. So often as a pastor, I have felt the need for words that have been missing from our churches' worship books: at the anniversary of a significant death; at the time of a community tragedy; or to acknowledge the ongoing life of a family who cares for a child who is chronically ill.

Everyone who worships regularly, as well as those who have fallen away from the church, feels emptiness in such moments. This emptiness longs for an appropriate word, a word, we might even dare to hope, from God, for us. In the communion service at Christmas time, Lutherans often use these words of praise:

> In the wonder and mystery of the Word made flesh
>   you [O God]
> have opened the eyes of faith
>   to a new and radiant vision of your glory;
> that, beholding the God made visible,
>   we may be drawn to love
>   the God whom we cannot see.[2]

Worship conveys this kind of power: Jesus Christ for us, God made visible in a human life; God invoked on our behalf; the steadfast love and mercy of God enacted for us in this particular moment that we might be drawn to faith. Here, now, Jesus Christ is incarnate—made flesh—for you. The body of Christ, broken for you. The blood of Christ, given for you.

New rituals come in various forms—from personal meditations that someone might use alone, to small gatherings of family or friends, to community-wide worship services in the midst of tragedy. They are at times personal or used alone, yet they always also bear the marks of community.

As we experience the love and mercy of God, we are reminded that we are in relationship with God and with each other and that God delivers us from sin and from bondage. These experiences invite us to place ourselves in service to God, in the midst of the world. I have found unexpected richness in creating new Christian rituals and have discovered new depth in my own understanding of Scripture and of various Christian worship traditions. My faith has deepened as I have witnessed the Holy Spirit at work in others' struggles with their faith and in the renewal they discover. This exchange between pastors and people in our congregation has borne fruit for the church, too. It has provided a way for people who have long been away from the Church to find a new place for themselves inside the Church: We have stood together in the presence of a living God.

I pray that you may also discover the rich rewards of this work in your ministry and that God's Word may speak through you to those living in the lands of silence.

PART ONE

UNDERSTANDING RITUAL

Chapter 1

How Can I Keep from Singing?
How New Rituals Come Alive

Shepherd me, O God,
beyond my wants
beyond my fears
from death into life.
Marty Haugen[1]

*O*n Palm Sunday in our church, we often have a dramatic reading of the passion story of Jesus in place of the sermon. Some years, in spite of our best efforts, the story remains at a distance. One year, it came alive for us in an unexpected way. An eighty-year-old member of our congregation read the part of Jesus, and as he began in a quavering voice I wondered if such an old one could convey Jesus to us. But something wonderful happened: he and the drummer and the dancer and all the voices of the congregation made the passion live not just *for* us, but *with* us and *through* us. At the end of the reading, the congregation sat in a profound, full silence, transformed. We felt deeply connected with one another. We were no longer a gathering of individuals, but children of God together, standing in the presence of a living God.

Ritual is like this. Its true purpose is not simply to mark an occasion, as a Palm Sunday reading might mark the anniversary of the death of Jesus in Judea two thousand years ago. Rather, by the power of the Holy Spirit, ritual is intended to affect us profoundly: We do not merely hear the story, we become the story. God speaks to us and through us.

For many contemporary people, even those actively involved in their churches, worship means boredom and tedium, even at times something false and meaningless—"empty ritual," the same order of things, an endless repetition. But form and structure are not inherently bad, and repetition, in itself, is not lifeless: they are the basis of poetry and prayer. The Lord's Prayer comes

3

to life anew in a crisis precisely because we have already repeated it hundreds of times. Similarly the order of a particular form is not necessarily deadening: bride and groom walk to the altar; they make promises to each other as family and friends bear witness; they pray for God's blessings no matter what may come. This is the very stuff of life. These actions—these forms—have existed for centuries. Repetition can be transformative. Form can be full of life and promise.

For me—and I hope for you—Christian ritual is an active and creative experience rooted deeply in Christian traditions *and* in the life of the community in which it takes place. Worship comes alive when it breathes with the life of particular people in a particular place, at this time and not some other. This is true whether you are considering the form of Sunday morning worship in a Baptist or Pentecostal congregation; the order of liturgical forms among Roman Catholics, Episcopalians, and Lutherans; or a ritual created for a one-time-only event. Ritual transforms us when it comes through our hands and is shaped by our hearts. When we give ourselves to ritual and to its preparation, we are often surprised to find God there with us, shepherding us.

WEAVING THE THREADS OF WORSHIP

I am a pastor, and I am also a weaver. I prepare my loom for weaving by tying the vertical warp threads to the back of the loom and threading them, one by one, through heddles. These are the foundation threads that will give the fabric stability. During the weaving, the heddles separate the warp threads, according to the steps of a pattern, to allow me to set the weft threads in place. These weft threads are the threads of movement, color, creativity—the threads that form the pattern that emerges as the cloth becomes whole. In the interplay of warp and weft—the play of the pattern across the underlying structure—the fabric is woven.

In the same way, a ritual's structure, its form or order, is the warp that provides its stability. Take, for example, the nightly ritual of saying grace. In our house, we eat together most nights. Night after night, even if we are not all together at any other time during the day, we sit around the table in our kitchen for a meal together. Some nights, we cannot fight back the chaos: one of us is too distracted; or someone arrives at the door; or our youngest is just too tired. But other nights a kind of magic happens. We join hands for a prayer, we sing together with food served before us on our plates, and time stands still. We are a family. We are essential to each other's lives, and God is with us. In this experience of grace, the threads that weave together to form ritual become apparent:

- Ritual is repetitive.
- Ritual is physical.
- Ritual is a time apart.
- Ritual makes a place for silence.
- Ritual invokes God.
- Ritual is not limited by what has come before.

RITUAL IS REPETITIVE

This is the warp thread of our grace, as it is of many rituals. We begin with something we already know. Our family learns new prayers for grace from time to time. Sometimes the prayer is a spoken, free prayer. But part of what takes us out of ourselves is that the opening part of the experience is now from memory. We need no papers, juggle no books. We are free to enter the experience and find depth and surprises there, because we already know where we start by heart.[2] Over, around, and through this repetition we weave the weft threads that follow.

RITUAL IS PHYSICAL

We are bodily present. In hunger, we savor the smells of food prepared. In weariness, we are grateful for food, companionship, and a time to sit. Ritual does not lift us out of our bodies, but through ritual we become vitally aware of life as it expresses itself in and through our bodies.

RITUAL IS A TIME APART

The prayer stops the clatter of dishes, the disparate rush of activities that brings us to the table. It brings us to a certain way of being in our bodies: attentive, focused, with hands joined, singing. Ritual opens us to the possibility of finding meaning in the ordinary events of our lives, of knowing that we live in the context of something larger than ourselves, in the presence of God.

RITUAL MAKES A PLACE FOR SILENCE

We come to silence before the prayer begins. Ritual is not *about* stillness and silence, but it makes a place for them in the rhythm of our days, a place for a power that reorders our lives. Reflecting on silence, theologian Mark Searle notes that the word "mystery" derives from the ancient Greek word μυστήριον, whose root means to close or cover the mouth: we are silent when words fail us, awestruck when we stand before forces greater than ourselves.[3] In silence we discover the limits of speech and of action.

RITUAL INVOKES GOD

Participating in ritual implies realities we cannot see. Ritual makes a place for our hearts to be turned back to the Holy One. Ritual welcomes God into all of our days' experiences. It shapes our attitudes after the pattern of Jesus, says Elaine Ramshaw, not by imputing feelings to us we do not feel, but by engaging us in actions we might not spontaneously perform. When we regularly give thanks, we may learn gratefulness.[4]

RITUAL IS NOT LIMITED BY WHAT HAS COME BEFORE

Because we know the words and enter the experience together, we are sometimes startled when someone—a child, perhaps—takes the lead or suggests a new verse or a new way of praying. When that happens, we grow together in the presence of a living God. We are transformed not simply because we are doing what we have done so many times before; we find wholeness in the surprising turns that come in the open spaces between the words we already know. We experience the power of the Holy Spirit to create faith, to establish and sustain community.

SEEING THE STRUCTURE AND MOVEMENT WITHIN RITUAL

Tom Driver observes that religious ritual moves between two poles: "At one pole, the paramount consideration is order, regularity, and limit. At the other, creativity and infusion of spirit."[5] Some faith traditions emphasize primarily the order; their leaders represent God, or mediate God, to the people. Other traditions emphasize primarily the infusion of Spirit; their leaders invoke God. All religious ritual includes both order/structure and movement/Spirit. It is partly through the interplay of these opposites—the stability of structure and the movement that flows within it—that ritual holds its richness and new life.

Worship leaders rarely ponder ritual's underlying structure or movement.

Familiar with our own congregation's worship life, with the range of experiences available within our denomination, rarely do we dig deeper. Yet there are underlying forms present in all kinds of ritual, across widely divergent Christian practices, moving between these poles of order/structure and movement/spirit.

For more occasional worship experiences—baptisms, weddings, blessings, and funerals, for instance—each has an underlying structure and movement that helps to reveal its meaning. Imagine for a moment a house blessing and a wedding. Both services move from beginning to middle to end; both involve Scripture readings, blessings, and prayers. But the services hold the pieces together in very different ways.

When we bless a dwelling, the structure of the ritual is focused on the place and those who live in it. The flow of the ritual moves participants through the rooms of the dwelling, with a Scripture reading and a prayer in each room or area. In contrast, the structure of the wedding service is focused on God's blessing of two who now also become one. Most of the wedding participants remain in the same physical place, while the bride and groom engage in powerful symbolic movement: they emerge singly from the congregation, from their families of origin, from their separate lives, to join together at the altar as a new couple. They speak their promises to each other aloud; prayers ask God's blessing; family and friends bear witness to the vows and add their own blessings.

When we are open to creating new worship experiences, the order and structure of a ritual can arise naturally out of the longings, experiences, and faith of those who will participate. One year during Lent, we invited the people involved in our church's outreach ministries to help us lead our midweek services. I worked with three women living in Deborah Place, our transitional residence for women and children who had been homeless. At first, the women reacted to the invitation with suspicion. None of them had been to church in years. They felt ashamed of their circumstances. They had not felt welcome in church during their years on the street and could not imagine that they had something to offer to a church's worship service.

We started by sitting together and talking. I asked them, What is it that carried you through your time on the streets? How did you manage when you did not have food for your children or a place to sleep? I was stunned by their answers. It had been more than ten years since any one of them had been inside a church. Yet each of them carried inside a Bible verse or a hymn that had sustained them through years of difficulty.

"I'm climbing up, on the rough side of the mountain," sang one woman.[6] "Trust in the LORD with all thine heart;" said the second, "and lean not unto thine own understanding" (Prov. 3:5 KJV). The third asked for a Bible, and she found this verse: "The eternal God *is thy* refuge, and underneath *are* the everlasting arms" (Deut. 33:27 KJV).

I had begun our planning session with a particular structure for worship in mind. Our Lenten services are usually a kind of evening prayer: responsive readings, psalms, and prayers, with a hymn near the beginning and one at the end. I had assumed we would follow that order. But different situations call forth different ritual structures and movement. As the women spoke, a new order—indeed, a new purpose—arose.

A simple service of praise and testimony presented itself to us, in thanksgiving to God who carries us through the difficult days of our lives. At the rite's heart was the women's testimony about what had carried them through their lives on the street. Each one told her own story and read her verse or sang her song. A simple meditation asked others to bring testimony about what had carried *them* through hard times. After the testimony, we sang together "Leaning on the Everlasting Arms," whose title and refrain paraphrase the verse from Deuteronomy, and prayed for people in all kinds of difficulty. The people in our church have talked about this Lenten service for years; and though I helped them hold it together, it was truly led by people who had been away from the church for much of their lives.

LEAVING OPEN SPACES FOR THE
HOLY SPIRIT TO ENTER

It's deceptively easy to understand the idea of structure and movement, but putting the idea into practice takes a little effort. That's because worship leaders often think they must plan everything out in advance "to make it work." But one secret to making ritual come alive lies not only in planning these "closed" portions, but also on leaving openings for the Holy Spirit to enter in, to surprise us with joy.

When the women of Deborah Place and I agreed to a certain structure to our worship service, we agreed on the form or order: How would we begin? Who would speak, and when? Where would the Scripture passages be read? Which ones? This structure was the warp, the set pieces, the parts that could be planned ahead, even rehearsed. Into these threads we wove our weft: our movement, the open portions that left space for spontaneous actions and speech and silence, and that allowed an opening for the prompting of the Holy Spirit. We left a place for the women's testimony, and their testimony became an invitation to the others present to know God in the hard places of their lives. We left silence where others present could add their prayers. And although we left these spaces open, had planned for them, we were still startled by the visit of the Holy Spirit. We had invited the women to help lead us, and at the same time, in our presumption, we did not imagine that their testimony of faith, fresh and new, would stir up in us such hope and faith!

Worship leaders of a ritual can't be aware of everything that participants bring with them to an occasion. Open spaces allow for some of what they bring to be incorporated into the worship experience, as it is appropriate. These open spaces may include prayers with space for participants to speak; silence; a time for personal testimony; extemporaneous reflections on someone's life; or comments on the meaning of a name, a place, a community, or a person's experience.

In the ritual for use after a miscarriage or stillbirth (see pp. 127–34), the parents are given the opportunity to speak about why they chose a certain name for their child, what the name means in the context of their family, and, by extension, what they had hoped for in their child. The parents should certainly be given a chance to think ahead about whether or not they will speak during the rite and, if they do, what they might say. They may even write out their thoughts in advance. But there is no telling what will happen among those gathered when the parents share the name, and when silence is left to hear and to respond to them.

Ritual should not be completely scripted in advance. Participants may well experience the presence of God in the planned sections of a rite. But the open sections provide the space and possibility that participants might be carried by the Spirit to a place where they didn't know they needed to go. Consider, for example, a liturgy for people struggling to overcome addiction. One person's testimony might lead the preacher to reshape her message for the day, which could shift the character of the congregation's prayers, which could lead another person to find the courage to move from addiction into recovery. "Behold," says the apostle Paul; "now is the day of salvation" (2 Cor. 6:2 RSV).

EMBRACING CONTRADICTION AND AMBIVALENCE

One of ritual's greatest strengths is its capacity to help us embrace powerful and even contradictory emotions. Certain life experiences contain opposing forces. Ritual contains contradictory emotions because the circumstances of our lives often include contradictory needs. As we move from a loved home, we may simultaneously feel a deep sense of loss and a sense of hopeful anticipation for the next phase of our life. At the death of a loved one, we need both to mourn the loss of someone close and also to celebrate what that life has meant to us: we know both sorrow and joy. At a community ritual commemorating youth killed violently on the streets, we may want both to cry out against injustice and to sing praises about God's presence with us through the most difficult days of our lives.

At the outset, it may appear inappropriate, if not offensive, to include perpetrators of sexual abuse in a healing ritual for those who have been violated. It probably would be unwise to have the abusers present at the service, and it is unlikely that they would want to come. But while the main focus of the service is on God's power to heal people who have been victims of abuse, Christian faith also follows Jesus as he walks among tax collectors and sinners. Our faith requires some acknowledgment of the humanity and needs of people who abuse others. A healing ritual for those who have been abused might well include prayers for the abusers: that they may be responsible for their actions and that they may know the mercy of God for their own healing.

Ritual can also help us handle ambivalence, the experience of feeling pulled in two opposing directions at one time. At age eighteen, for example, many teens are eager to get away from home, to become more self-sufficient. Yet, at the same time, they are often anxious about what the change will mean for their relationship with their parents, about how they will do on their own, about setting out to a place where they know no one. Teen bravado may make it hard for them to express their fear even as it gives them the courage and will to step away from home, parents, and the security of what they have known.

In *Ritual and Pastoral Care,* Elaine Ramshaw describes how ritual can handle such ambivalence by making space for the emotions on both sides, even while it emphasizes one side, a "preferred" emotion. For instance, when a teen's family creates a ritual that affirms his or her value to them, the ritual anchors the teen securely in love. It can create enough safety for the teen to name anxieties about leaving home and for the teen's parents to pray for his or her growth in responsibility. Fear and anxiety are still present, but security and love temper them and are the stronger message conveyed.

Ritual can leave space for a symbolic expression of feeling, says Ramshaw, by calling forth from Scripture a wide range of voices for calling on God. We may praise God or ask for mercy, but, like Abraham, we may also bargain with God. We may "mourn like Rachel, protest like Job, press our case beyond a dismissal like the Syrophoenician woman, or cry out of our abandonment like Jesus."[7]

In true ambivalence, we freeze, unable to move, for the strength of the opposing forces is roughly equal. When, through ritual, we can hear our own voices in the words Scripture uses to speak to God, we become empowered to acknowledge what is hard for us, yet we are free to move forward because we are securely anchored in the love of God that is more powerful than the difficulty we face.

HUMAN NEEDS PLACED IN THE LIGHT OF GOD

Ritual acknowledges our needs and losses by placing them in the context of God's redemptive love and care for the world and for us. Praise for God that stands alone without considering our particularity is abstract and hollow. In the Old Testament book that bears his name, Job suffered a series of tragedies. His friends respond to him with pious platitudes. Finally, in exasperation, Job says, "How then will you comfort me with empty nothings?" (Job 21:34). Blessings alone in worship can be empty nothings when they leave no space for us to name our needs before God. A retirement farewell, for example, is usually not simply a time of joy about work well done. Often it also marks a major shift in one's life and includes experiences of sorrow and loss. Joy and sorrow, praise and petition, stand together. Similarly, when we gather in worship to acknowledge the loss of a child, ritual provides a fitting vehicle by which to lay our grief, anger, or despair before God. Ironically, it is through entering the depth of our own needs that, with the appropriate framework and support, we may discover lips of praise for God even in our sorrow.

It is not coincidental that many words used to describe our need to be in relationship with God—"hunger" or "longing," for example—are first expressions of physical human needs. Biblical faith allows us to acknowledge even the parts of ourselves that make us tremble with fear. Like generations before us, Scripture shows us how to lay our needs before God.

From that ritual can follow: ritual's character and movement is evoked through particular needs. Human need is never the sole focus of Christian worship; but particular needs are never completely absent. Sunday morning worship allows for the expression of participants' needs at least in the prayers. Special services allow for more focused attention on a variety of needs and the ways God addresses those needs in a wider variety of contexts than is possible in regular weekly worship services.

What makes the expression of need Christian is that the need is allowed to stand in the light of the Word of God and of God's redeeming work in Jesus

Christ. By attending to real human needs as people experience them, even the most difficult moments of our lives can draw us to know and to praise God.

When we place our needs and our losses in God's hands, we acknowledge that we are not left alone during the most difficult days of our lives. When we place them in God's hands *through ritual,* we enact the story of salvation anew in our own place.

FOR FURTHER READING

Tom F. Driver. *Liberating Rites: Understanding the Transformative Power of Ritual.* Boulder, CO: Westview Press, 1998.

Gordon W. Lathrop. *Holy People: A Liturgical Ecclesiology.* Minneapolis: Augsburg Fortress, 1999.

Elaine Ramshaw. *Ritual and Pastoral Care.* In series Theology and Pastoral Care. Edited by Don S. Browning. Philadelphia: Fortress Press, 1987.

Victor Turner. *The Forest of Symbols: Aspects of Ndembu Ritual.* Ithaca, NY: Cornell University Press, 1967.

Chapter 2

Listening for God's Word:
Characteristics of Ritual in New Contexts

> *The angel of God called to Hagar from heaven,*
> *and said to her, "What troubles you, Hagar?*
> *Do not be afraid; for God has heard the voice*
> *of [your son] where he is."*
>
> *Gen. 21:17*

A ritual is performed at a certain time and place; it is repetitive in its parts
and movement, and is known deeply from the inside. So how, then, can we
use ritual in new contexts, to mark places we may visit only once in our whole
lives: the death of a child, a community tragedy, a marriage or divorce, the
breaking up of a loved home near the end of life?

The answer, I believe, is to draw in part from more common ritual experiences. In this way, the occasional rituals contain enough that is familiar to
carry us through an unfamiliar experience. Prayer and praise, or silence,
familiar to us from Sunday worship, may anchor the new rite; participants
may speak the prayers in a form they already know; or the new rite may
include psalms, prayers, or songs that are themselves known by heart.

In any case, my own ministry has taught me that satisfying, new Christian
rituals can be created and can become the meeting ground where the Word of
God speaks to people's physical, psychological, and spiritual needs. These rituals are successful when they allow participants to encounter the presence of
God, to find healing, to grieve, to celebrate, to discover or nurture faith, or to
be moved on to a new stage of life.

No matter the situation, new rituals that work well contain these characteristics:

- Ritual grows out of a particular need.
- Ritual bears God's Word of redemption for someone in need.

13

- Ritual conveys its deepest meanings through the use of symbols.
- Ritual is by nature communal.
- Ritual's meaning and movement is enhanced by music.

It's not that paying attention to these elements of ritual will work magic all by themselves: God's presence does that! But when we pay attention to these things, they become like building blocks for creating new rituals. Together they create a space in which we may experience the wonder of God's presence with us.

Most of all, when we think about creating new rituals, we must *pay attention* as we ask, What is the need? How is it expressed? What parts of Scripture and tradition, what Word from God, speak to this need? What symbolizes the need? What symbolizes the Word from God? What signs of Christian community can be made visible for people who are isolated? What music lifts our voices in praise? At every stage of preparation, creating new rituals involves learning to pay attention more closely.

RITUAL GROWS OUT OF A PARTICULAR NEED

God's Holy Spirit ministers to people in surprising ways, sometimes before we know how to ask. Our desire in creating new rituals is that God might also act through us and the worship experiences we lead to bring a healing word for participants. New rituals like the ones found in this book are not created in the abstract. They grow out of particular human needs. Thus before you can bring the need into a setting where the Word of God may speak, heal, and transform, first you must listen for that need, individual or communal, and understand it. Creating a ritual that works, even for a "standard" rite like a funeral, requires those who lead the service to listen for the needs of those who will participate. The need to listen is intensified in a situation in which you want to create rituals where there have been none.

When Fred and Kathy Powell's son Josh had pneumonia one winter, his hospitalization and recovery took much longer than they expected. He suffered with a rare degenerative neurological disorder. The illness that winter triggered a period of physical decline. Weeks turned into months, and their son could not be taken out of the house. Their life as a family shifted radically as they took turns staying home with him. Though they were able to continue working, they began to feel more and more isolated from the other activities of their life, including church. Yet many people hesitated to visit, not wanting to intrude. Sometime in the months it took to adapt to the new circumstances of their life, I began to talk with them about what kind of visits from others could be supportive. I began our conversation by first listening to their needs. Then we considered what kind of ritual might help to provide healing.

Sometimes we need to discover new ways to listen in order to deepen our understanding of life situations we have never encountered. If, for example, you have never before met someone struggling with addiction, or in recovery from addiction, you may miss some of the cues that are obvious to a more experienced listener. To deepen your listening skills and as background preparation for your conversation with someone about a possible new ritual, you might find another person with a similar experience to talk with or read some of the many printed materials available.

Before a friend asked me to write a ritual to help her prepare for the surgery that would remove a breast because of cancer, I had never talked with anyone about the experience of losing a breast. I found it helpful to spend an afternoon in a large bookstore, perusing the many offerings in the women's health section. I found several diaries, first-person accounts, written by women who had had mastectomies. I discovered that women have many different experiences with breast cancer, and even with mastectomy, and that there wasn't one "right" way of thinking about it. The books focused my listening, deepened my understanding, and allowed me to go back to my friend to hear more specifically what she felt she needed for that moment in her life. Talking with others who had experienced breast cancer could have provided another way.

Our Listening and God's Hearing

Let's consider how listening to someone might help to shape a ritual.

Joyce was returning to church after forty years: What sort of ritual would speak to her need? First, listen to her story.

Most of the years she'd been away from the church, she had struggled with alcoholism without being able to acknowledge it. As the years passed, she began to believe that it did not matter if she lived or died. The night her problems became a crisis, she was one week into a month-long program at a rehabilitation hospital. It was not going well. Joyce felt that the counselor assigned to her treated her in a demeaning way, but she felt weak and angry and unable to speak adequately for herself. She planned, instead, to walk out of the program.

On her way out of the building, as Joyce passed the nurses' station, a nurse saw how upset she was and invited her to talk. Joyce was able to express her anger for the first time. With the nurse's support, Joyce also spoke with the head counselor, who invited Joyce to tell him what was going on with her. For an hour and a half a tumult of her feelings poured out, and for the first time in her life, she said exactly what she meant without censoring herself. She spoke the truth of her life as best she knew it, and they listened. When she was finished, she got up and went to bed.

To be heard is a profoundly holy experience.

Because the nurse and the head counselor listened that night, Joyce discovered that what she did, what she said, what she believed, mattered. Because they heard her, Joyce felt stronger. She was able to stay for the remaining weeks of her treatment, even staying in the group with the counselor she had found so difficult.

When Joyce looks back on that June night, she knows that she stood on holy ground. She turned the corner and moved into recovery. By the grace of God, she has never turned back. Over the years of her recovery, Joyce realized that before she could speak for herself, she needed someone to listen to her. She came to understand that as others listened to her, *God* heard her cry.

RITUAL BEARS GOD'S WORD OF REDEMPTION

When worship leaders hold a particular need clearly in focus, the next task of ritualizing becomes a second kind of listening: listening for how God's Word speaks to *this* need. Worship leaders explore the rich store of Scripture and Christian tradition, for a Word from God to speak to this particular need.

One way to name the character of Christian faith is to recognize that people want their own particular experiences and stories to be connected to the great biblical stories and to the life of faith in Jesus: stories of bondage and freedom, of sin and forgiveness, of regret and new beginnings, of doubt and faith, of death and new life. We want to know God in and through the days and the experiences of our own lives and of the life of our community. An older woman in our church experienced a kind of personal transformation as she remembered the passion story of Jesus.

Lying on her bed in a rehabilitation hospital, Margaret told me about an aide who had helped her get ready for bed the night before. It was Maundy Thursday, the night the church remembers the Last Supper of Jesus, when he began the meal by washing his disciples' feet (John 13:1–11). Margaret is a very private and self-reliant person. Like many of us in her circumstances, she found it hard to need so much care. "It was very moving," she said. "The woman came in the room, got a basin ready, took the heavy stockings off of me, got a cloth, and washed my feet."

In the action of the woman's washing, in the way she held the towel, Margaret felt Jesus visiting her. By Jesus' presence, Margaret was able to receive the help she needed more willingly. Understanding herself within the biblical story lightened the part of her burden that had to do with her difficulty receiving from others. When we come to know biblical stories in this way, we sometimes find ourselves living inside their rhythms and movements. The woman's washing placed Margaret within the story of Jesus' washing the disciples' feet before the Last Supper, which reminded her that Jesus was with her. Placed by the experience within a greater story, though it was still hard for her, Margaret came to understand that receiving care is time spent in the presence of God. In a difficult time, God's Holy Spirit revived her!

When creating a ritual, we want to choose biblical texts, readings, and prayers that speak to a particular need, as John 13 spoke to Margaret. Through Scripture and the resources of Christian worship traditions, participants may come to know themselves as both loved and redeemed by God.

We can now see that the first two characteristics of new rituals are interconnected: worship leaders listen for a need to understand it and for a Word from God to speak to that need. Thus new rituals place a particular need in the light of the Word of God. "Your word, [O God]," says the psalmist, "is a lamp to my feet and a light to my path" (Ps. 119:105).

RITUAL CONVEYS ITS DEEPEST MEANINGS
THROUGH THE USE OF SYMBOLS

How, then, shall we embody the Word of God in ritual?

All rituals involve at least one symbol. In fact, ethnographer Victor Turner describes a symbol as the "smallest unit of ritual."[1] In some churches, when someone is baptized, he or she is dressed in a new white garment, a sign of new life in Christ. The newly baptized may be marked with the sign of the cross on the forehead with scented oil ("You belong to Jesus Christ") or given a candle ("Let the light of Christ now shine in what you do and say"). Similarly, a newly married husband and wife wear rings—unbroken circles—as a reminder both of God's unending love for them and of the promises they have made to each other to be faithful until death parts them.

Symbols convey meaning that is deeper than words. They offer us a flash of understanding that goes beyond the cognitive mind to make visible what is invisible. A symbol's power to speak to us deep inside can be seen in Sarah's story:

Sarah was only four years old when she experienced physical symptoms serious enough to warrant a day trip to the hospital for general anesthesia and tests. Her parents were terrified. They wanted to be calm, but they knew she saw their fear.

Active members of an Episcopal church, the family knew their priest well. She came to visit the day before the trip to the hospital. After a little while with her parents, the priest moved into the next room to see Sarah. Somewhere during their play, Sarah's mother watched the priest take off her cross, the one she had been given at her ordination, the one she always wore. She said to Sarah, "Once before, there was a child who had surgery. He liked having this cross with him while he was in the hospital. It seemed to help. Would you like to borrow this cross?" When Sarah said she did, the priest placed it around her neck and told her, "If you get worried or scared, you can hold tight on this cross. And one more thing: Would you watch your parents? If they seem worried or scared, you might think of sharing the cross with them."

At some place deep inside, deeper than words go, giving Sarah that cross speaks of God's love: Love that finds her irreplaceable. Love enough that Jesus would die for her. Love and reassurance enough to carry her through whatever troubles would come.

Scripture also conveys meaning through the use of symbols. When the Hebrew people wandered in the wilderness before entering the Promised Land, they despaired that God was not with them. The Lord appeared to them in a pillar of cloud and fire. By this visual sign, they were shown what they could not otherwise perceive. When the Israelites were about to be carried off into exile in a foreign land, the prophet Jeremiah bought a plot of land as a sign: God would eventually bring them back home to their own land. After Jesus' resurrection, his early followers held their possessions in common as an outward sign that their lives and all that they had belonged to God.

Elaine Ramshaw has observed that when a new ritual works, it is functioning symbolically. The ritual shows participants something about themselves, about their place in the world, about their relationships with their community, about the presence of God.[2] A church developed a rite of passage as part of its confirmation weekend. The rite of passage included a spiritual journey enacted in a darkened sanctuary with Christian symbols writ large: water, bread and wine, the cross. The teens being confirmed walked through the sanctuary with a congregational sponsor, received a blessing from their parents, and were clothed in white capes recalling their baptisms. In churches that use them, baptismal garments are symbolic of the person's "putting on Christ" and show forth each one's beauty and worth before God.

The overused claim "All are welcome" was in this case accurate and true.

One teen's awkward movements made the symbol of the baptismal garments work for me. Suffering from cerebral palsy, he could neither read nor write. As the class prepared for confirmation with written statements of faith, one of the pastors examined him orally. When the pastor discovered that the boy knew Jesus and was ready to take on greater responsibility in the church, which was that congregation's requirements for becoming confirmed, he was confirmed like all the others. That night, he walked the same spiritual journey as his classmates, but with a different gait. The symbol of the garments revealed truth as we watched his participation. He belonged to Jesus Christ together with his classmates, across lines that often divide us:

> The eye cannot say to the hand, "I have no need of you," nor again the head to the feet, "I have no need of you." On the contrary, the members of the body that seem to be weaker are indispensable. (1 Cor. 12:21–22)

> . . . for all of you are one in Christ Jesus. (Gal. 3:28)

The teen's body, his movements, also worked symbolically in the confirmation ritual, showing participants the arms of Jesus wide enough to receive him as a peer to his classmates. In fact, every ritual involves us physically, and our bodies also speak symbolically. Some ritual situations call for special sensitivity about how our bodies communicate.

A person who enters a nursing home, for instance, often does so out of necessity, not desire: his body is frail or failing; her mind is no longer capable enough to manage alone; a loved one who provided care is no longer able to do so. Depending on how one "stages" participants, a ritual of house blessing in a nursing-home room can convey either pity or blessing. Pity is evoked when the disability predominates in the ritual: when the person lies in bed while everyone else stands, when he has no space to speak a word, or where there is no sign of his life beyond his illness.

In contrast, a ritual that attends to basic questions about participants' bodies—visualizing, that is, how our bodies are working symbolically in that setting—will convey instead a sense of blessing. If the nursing-home resident must remain in bed, can the bed be raised so that he rests at eye level, with other participants seated around his bed in chairs? Including signs of the resident's life and interests—a favorite painting, pictures of events with family or friends, a piece of needlepoint that she has created—will convey personhood beyond a failing body.

Symbols can also exert their power in ways that undermine a ritual. When Nicholas Wolterstorff's son died in a mountain climbing accident, his funeral helped Wolterstorff feel both the reality of the death and the affirmation that death was not the only reality. He writes that although he dreaded the thought of the funeral, the actual experience "gave rest to [his] soul."

Those gathered used numerous symbols in the course of the service. A handmade shroud, lilies, music, Eucharist: each symbol played a role in making the funeral life-giving. But during the service, the use of another symbol became more troubling. Wolterstorff wrote,

> Then we left, I carrying the resurrection candle, Claire beside me, followed by the family and the coffin.
>
> The candle was still burning firmly and brightly as the people began pressing round. The undertakers stirred to take the coffin away. What am I to do now, blow out this symbol of the resurrection of my son? Why had no one foreseen the impossible pain of this the final act?
>
> "But it's only a candle."
> "No, it's more than a candle."[3]

For assistance in naming symbols that work for you, choosing appropriate symbols for a ritual, and charting symbolic action, see the exercises in chapter 7 (pp. 173–77). As you search for symbols to use in your own rituals, by all means use those that have been established over time and are grasped quickly by participants. But remember also to look for symbolism where you might not expect to find it for use in the church's ministry: in the tattoos and piercings of teens pushing toward adulthood and searching to exhibit mastery over their own bodies; in photographs of the ocean hanging on someone's wall, reminders of sun and water and rest; in the music played as people gather for a funeral, favorites of the one who has died and reminders of the faith that sustained him. When the symbols that already function in people's lives are connected to a Word from God, they can be the most evocative of all.

RITUAL IS BY NATURE COMMUNAL

Those who share ritual together become a living connection to the wider life of a Christian community. Henry was an old man. He had spent almost all of his life in our congregation. In the last months of his life he was too frail to be alone and went to live with his daughter three hours away. I wanted to see Henry settled with his daughter. I wanted to see him one last time before he died, so a member of the church and I made the trip together.

What gift could we take with us? we wondered. He wasn't the sort to enjoy flowers, and he could no longer read. We decided to make a tape of our Sunday worship service. For part of our visit, we sat and listened to the tape with him. Then we shared communion.

When he heard the congregation begin to sing the opening hymn, tears rolled from Henry's eyes—tears both of joy and of sorrow. He who had worshiped every Sunday of his life was brought together again with his church. We were reminded that the worship of the church belongs to the whole church, as Dietrich Bonhoeffer observed sixty years ago when he was isolated in prison. He wrote, "When we hear the song, it is the voice of the church singing, and you, as a member of the church, may share its song."[4] Short of bringing Henry back for a Sunday, we could offer no finer gift than bringing the church's singing to him. Bringing another member of the congregation to share the visit and listening together to the whole congregation at worship became visible signs that we all belonged, together, to a people, the church.

Some people in our communities are invisible, and often their invisibility is a sign of isolation, which arises from a variety of causes. Sometimes people isolate themselves in embarrassment or shame—perhaps their marriage is crumbling, their addiction is spinning out of control, they are struggling with depression or other mental illness, or sexual issues are involved. Isolation can creep up gradually as someone ages or experiences an extended illness, their own or a loved one's. In an experience like miscarriage, isolation can happen because the experience is quite difficult for relatives and friends also of childbearing age. Unconsciously, they often turn away because of the vulnerability it makes them feel.

These situations require heightened pastoral sensitivity. Folks from an older generation in the congregation might visit with couples who miscarry, for instance, or people years into recovery might have a special ministry with those still struggling in active addiction. Others just need some way of staying connected to a congregation's life. In either case, ritual may help participants discover or strengthen their connections with others.

Human connections are essential both to life and to our life together in the body of Christ. The sculptor Auguste Rodin created numerous pieces involving human hands. One striking sculpture called "The Cathedral" is created of just two hands, loosely connected, openness between them, fingers pointing toward heaven. Their presence together seems to create divine space within it. One can view the sculpture for a long time before realizing that it is crafted of two right hands. Christians cannot be Christians alone.

The circumstances of our lives do sometimes isolate us, though, and sometimes in discouragement or despair we isolate ourselves. Ritual provides the opportunity to make evident the connections of Christian community, especially for those who feel isolated. Even when a ritual is performed alone, like the meditations offered in chapter 4 for people recovering from sexual abuse (pp. 83–91), participants are connected to believers in other places by praying the psalms, which are used daily by millions of people around the world.

These connections flow in two directions: through physical symbols and by human contact from the congregation to the one who is isolated and back again. This happens most fruitfully when the people involved in a new ritual already belong to a congregation, even if they are currently isolated from it, although other forms of community, like connections with former coworkers, neighbors, friends, and family, also might provide an appropriate context.

For example, Irene needed to know that she still mattered to her congregation, though illness had kept her away from worship for many years. Lou Gehrig's disease—amyotrophic lateral sclerosis (ALS)—had progressively narrowed the boundaries of her life, robbing her of mobility, the ability to eat regular foods, and hence many of the most obvious signs of community.

Irene faced her disability with amazing patience. One exception, however, was her frustration about knitting. ALS had taken the use of one hand. Eventually she found that if she used very fine yarns with small knitting needles, she could knit with the other hand. The problem was that fine yarns work well for knitting baby clothing, but there were no more babies in her family. When she talked about her dilemma with me on a pastoral visit, she wasn't expecting a solution, but I saw a possible connection. I asked her, "Could you knit for the babies at St. Michael's?"

Some months later, Irene could barely contain her excitement. She had finished knitting a baby cap for a little girl. With her daughter she wove pink ribbon through the loops at the neckline. They wrapped it in tissue paper and placed it in a gift bag. That Sunday we baptized an infant named Grace. (We have lots of babies. They belong to us together.) We incorporated Irene's gift into the service as the congregation's gift to its newest sister in Christ. Such a gift presentation is not a standard part of our church's baptismal rite, but we adapted the ritual to create something new, thus making our connections with Irene visible to the whole community.

We wished that Irene could have witnessed the baptism in person. But it was better that she had a role in the baptismal ritual, as the one who prepared the congregation's gift, than that she had no visible tie to her congregation's ongoing worship life. We hear the voice of the apostle Paul again reminding us: "The members of the body that seem to be weaker are indispensable" (1 Cor. 12:22).

Physical signs and tokens of the wider community can also be incorporated into new rituals. Elaine Ramshaw tells of a rabbi who bought a six-foot prayer shawl in Israel. On occasion, when he prays for or blesses someone from the congregation, he wraps the person in the shawl as a visible sign both of God's enfolding love and of the wider community to which the person belongs.[5] Worship articles—candlesticks from the altar, the church's Bible, a tape or CD from a regular worship service or of the pastor preaching, special communion vessels—all are physical reminders of the wider community, as are members of the community themselves. If someone from the congregation is to visit with a minister, be careful to get the approval of the one to be visited; worship leaders need to attend to the needs for privacy of the person for whom the new ritual is created.

The Fellowship Meal with the Family of a Chronically Ill or Disabled Child in chapter 3 (pp. 53–55) provides an example of how making community connections visible through ritual flows in both directions. Members of the wider community bring food for the meal and a candle from the church's altar. They sing a hymn and offer a place for the family to speak about the struggles they face because of their child's illness or disability. Then together they make an ornament for the church's Christmas tree. The people who brought the food carry the ornament back to the tree in the church's sanctuary and offer a prayer for the child and his family during the regular Sunday worship service. Back and forth, a community's connections are made more visible and ritual strengthens the bonds of community.

RITUAL'S MEANING AND MOVEMENT IS ENHANCED BY MUSIC

In Elie Wiesel's novel *The Oath*, Rebbe exclaims that song carries humanity to the highest palace, influencing, from there, the universe and its prisons. "Sing," says the Rebbe, "and you shall defeat death, sing and you shall disarm the foe."[6] In joy and in sorrow, in conflict and in making peace, in lament and in praise, music draws our hearts to God.

Even people who can no longer remember the faces of their children or their own names can sometimes sing a beloved hymn with others. A person in crisis may find that the words of a song sung at home in childhood come back unexpectedly, binding the generations across time and distance.

When doctors were trying to determine if the irregularity they observed in Mary's breast was cancer, she underwent a procedure called wire localization. It was a painful procedure, performed while her breast was held tightly by the mammogram machine. The whole experience was frightening, but in the middle of the procedure she began to hear sung to her the Taizé "Kyrie"— in harmony! *Lord, have mercy.* Calmness overtook her.

When creating new rituals, we can use music from a wide range of musical styles. One pastor, for example, dealt with a terrible tragedy. His adolescent son's best friend had been handling a gun, not knowing it was loaded. The gun went off; the boy died. The pastor was scout leader for both boys. The friend's family had no church home, so he agreed to do the funeral. He talked with me about how he had put the service together.

We talked about passages from Scripture, about grief, about his own loss. He was satisfied with how he had been able to bear witness to God, in the midst of the tragedy, except when it came to the music. For, of all the hymns he knew, he found none that could bear the weight of such anguish. They opted for instrumental music instead. Instrumental music is a fitting choice, but there are songs—words and music—that would work. In Negro spirituals, for example, anguish and faith are often intertwined. Music capable of bearing the weight of slavery can also bear the weight of contemporary tragedy. The spirituals draw us to Jesus, who has stood in a place resembling where we now stand, who can redeem even this moment. I can hear the strains of the spiritual "Nobody Knows the Trouble I've Seen," which ends with this line: "Glory Hallelujah!" Great sorrow is uttered, but in the next breath, so is faith and confidence in God's power. If the grieving ones feel only doubt or despair in the midst of their grief, the congregation that surrounds them bears witness to the presence of God for them. The congregation sings the faith for them, until they can pick up the song again for themselves.

Biblical psalms of lament are more familiar to some than the spirituals, and many worship traditions set psalms to music. The lament psalms speak well in the midst of tragedy. Some even rail at God, or give voice to despair: "My God, my God, why have you forsaken me?" (Ps. 22:1). Such psalms might also be spoken to background music that evokes an appropriate mood. If these musical suggestions fall outside your experience, consider who in your community might lead the music in a new ritual or who might offer their music as a part of it.

In these introductory chapters, we have considered the characteristics of ritual in new contexts and the ways that ritual comes alive. Both discussions have called for an openness to considering how the church extends its ministries through creating new rituals. What follows now are a wide range of examples of new rituals, grouped together by common themes. Each chapter and each ritual introduces readers to an area of ministry where a new ritual might enhance a congregation's ministry and pastoral care. Pastoral stories introduce both the rituals and the chapters of rituals.

I invite you to enter the chapters that follow with an open heart so that you might consider how to carry a word from God, embodied in ritual, to the places of need where your ministry carries you. God bless your going out, in Jesus' name. Amen.

FOR FURTHER READING

Ronald Grimes. *Marrying and Burying: Rites of Passage in a Man's Life.* Boulder, CO: Westview Press, 1995.

Evan Imber-Black and Janine Roberts. *Rituals for Our Times: Celebrating, Healing, and Changing Our Lives and Our Relationships.* San Francisco: HarperCollins Publishers, 1992.

Evan Imber-Black, Janine Roberts, and Richard Whiting, editors. *Rituals in Families and Family Therapy.* New York: W. W. Norton & Company, 1988, 2003.

Rabbi Debra Orenstein, editor. *Lifecycles: Jewish Women on Life Passages and Personal Milestones.* Volume 1. Woodstock, VT: Jewish Lights Publishing, 1994.

PART TWO

NEW RITES
FOR CHRISTIAN WORSHIP

Chapter 3

Ritual Signs of New Life
and New Community

Remember not the former things,
nor consider the things of old.
Behold, I am doing a new thing;
now it springs forth, do you not perceive it?
Isaiah 43:18–19 RSV

*C*ommunity can be built in any environment. The teen came in and sat down to wait his turn. He was early for his voice lesson. He sat and watched the woman sing who had her lesson before him, then she watched him start his lesson. Their teacher is a professional singer and voice teacher for the operatic stage. Along the way, she also came to work with children with developmental disabilities. The teen was one of those children. Their teacher was with the boy in exactly the same way she was with the woman before him, or with others who were preparing for a performance at a famous opera house. She helped each of them connect with the music and with themselves. The boy's singing would never take him to the professional stage, but something wondrous happened when he sang.

His teacher had him warm up his voice with scales. His whole body came alive. He seemed to become himself in a more complete way. There was an enormous joy as he sang. He loved what he was doing. With joy he was connected to the music, to his teacher, and to himself.

When I speak of new life and new community, I am thinking of experiences like these. It is the moment when new life breaks forth unexpectedly— here, an experience of joy, wholeness, and connection. Filmmaker Ilana Trachtman articulated the surprise of new life after she filmed a community's celebration of a boy's bar mitzvah. The boy has Down Syndrome, yet his whole community basks in his light, for he prays with such fervent devotion to God. Trachtman said, "It never occurred to me that we need to include somebody for our sake—that they benefit from [the inclusion], but we do, too."[1] Without realizing it, Trachtman had expected little from such a boy. Her realization of her own need for community *with him* is another experience where new life and new community becomes visible, ordered by love and joy.

There is a deep inner connection between the child of God held secure in God's love and the discovery of new community. For the one who knows he is loved is secure enough to allow space for another to be *as she is,* and so there is a place for each one, together.

Jesus gathered people together in this way, making a space for them, cherishing them, giving them to each other: the woman who anointed him for burial ("Leave her alone," Jesus told Judas; John 12:7); sinners at his table with him (Matt. 11:19); from the cross, giving his mother and the beloved disciple to each other (John 19:26–27).

Ritual seems uniquely able both to call new communities into being and to be a sign of new life in God—because it is public and communal; because it uses symbols and symbolic action as its tools; because it allows space for the Holy Spirit of God to move among us. I have been a witness of these things, and I'm guessing that you have, too.

Families of homicide victims find each other and celebrate Christmas together, or members of a choir find a place within themselves to nurture their connections with a family whose child is chronically ill or disabled. This new life and new community in Christ is the sustenance of friends supporting one among them who is treated unjustly at work. New life is evident when a place is made sacred again after its desecration by murder or rape and when an addict moves into recovery and stays there, perhaps after years of trying and failing.

The rituals in this section are both markers of new life and agents for creating new community. In doing them, the new life of this kind of community is called forth, nurtured, and sustained. The rituals do not work in isolation. They require sensitivity and mature insight about how people might come together; attention to the questions of when, how, and where to do them; and careful consideration regarding who should initiate them. Yet when these rituals, and others like them, work, they bring with them the new community for which their participants long.

VISIBLE SIGNS OF SUPPORT DURING
TIMES OF ADVERSITY

Hear, O Israel: The LORD is our God, the LORD alone. . . .
Keep these words . . . in your heart. . . .
Bind them as a sign on your hand,
fix them as an emblem on your forehead,
and write them on the doorposts of your house.
Deut. 6:4, 6, 8–9

Rachel Naomi Remen, a physician, provides psychological support to those who are ill. For more than twenty years, she has offered a simple ritual to patients preparing for surgery for cancer or treatment through radiation or chemotherapy. She suggests that the patient gather close friends and family together the day before the procedure. It does not matter how many come but only that they are "those who are connected to them, through a bond of the heart." She asks the person to find an ordinary stone.

When the people gather, they sit in a circle and speak, in turn, holding the stone. Each tells the story of a crisis she or he faced and what personal quality helped carry them through. After naming the "quality of their strength, they speak directly to the person preparing for surgery or treatment, saying, 'I put determination into this stone for you,' or 'I put faith into this stone for you.' " The patient then carries the stone along into treatment, sometimes even taping it to a hand during surgery.

Remen notes that no one enters surgery or treatment "without the thoughts, hopes and prayers of many people going with them. The stone seems to make all that a little more plain to people. . . . Ritual is one of the oldest ways to mobilize the power of community for healing. It makes the caring of the community visible, tangible, real."[2]

For Christians, the messages of community are strengthened through a shared faith that can be articulated as support through difficult times. They bear the reminder that God is also near—as near as our foreheads or our doorposts—even when we can't perceive God's presence ourselves.

The ritual that follows arose as a woman struggled with a difficult job. She believed that she had been treated unfairly and that she had no recourse. She could hear echoes all around her: *There is no place for you here.* It was a poisonous environment, and not simply for her. There were signs of dysfunction long before she arrived.

As she searched for other work, the woman could barely stand to set foot on the property of her employer. Yet for reasons economic and professional, she endured harsh working conditions until she was free to leave. In the intervening time, in conversation with a friend, she devised a ritual to help carry her through her remaining weeks. The thought came to her: "Write this down: 'There is a real problem here, and it's not of your making.'" She asked friends if they agreed with her reading of her work situation, and when they did, she asked if they would sign their names to the paper where she wrote it down.

The woman had used a small piece of paper, and she expected her friends to sign just their first names, like on a greeting card. But the first friend signed it with her whole name, as though it were a legal document. The others followed suit. She put the paper in a locket and wore it around her neck. It carried her through the difficult days and bore a mighty weight for her. Symbolically it said, "The people at your job have made a judgment about you that is unfair. They would have you believe that you are the problem, but problems existed here long before you came. Remember your value before us, and before God. Even in this time of your suffering, the Kingdom of Heaven is at hand for you. The Word of God, for you, is near at hand with you, to sustain you. Hold onto these things." (Matt. 3:2; Deut. 30:14)

Her friends expressed their care for her visibly, through a ritual act of signing their names on a paper where she wrote the truth as she understood it. The ritual act of wearing the locket held her friends near her as she suffered, and it reminded her of God's presence with her to deliver her.

You may discover other such situations in your ministry. The ritual could work in other circumstances where a person feels isolated in the midst of a crowd, mistreated, or in the midst of a difficult transition.

ᔕᔕᔕᔕᔕᔕᔕ

AMULET: A VISIBLE SIGN WHEN WORK IS DIFFICULT

Finding oneself in a job that becomes impossible, or being terminated, or being downsized out of a job are terribly isolating experiences. Yet the experiences, though varied, share this in common: they tear down a person's sense of worth and well-being, even if it is widely recognized that the person is caught in circumstances beyond his or her control. Such circumstances can also be complicated by difficult working relationships, misunderstandings, or legal action.

Though friends may offer support in various ways, this ritual focuses simply on providing moral support through difficulty at work, for as long as it lasts.

An amulet is a charm, often inscribed with a spell or a symbol, that wearers believe will protect them, as from disease, or during wartime. Christians don't use magic spells but do sometimes need physical reminders of God's presence with them. As you plan this ritual with a participant, consider what item might comfortably be carried at work, whether a locket, a wallet, or a message on a cell phone.

The person seeking support should invite a small group of friends and family. They should gather at home, or in a place that affords privacy. A small chapel at church might work well. Either a pastor or spiritual friend could lead the ritual.

Should it be clear that a person's actions have caused him or her to be fired for just cause, and should the person desire to confess his or her shortcomings to God and make a change, it would be possible to begin this ritual with an order of confession and forgiveness. Select an appropriate order from your church's worship book and make that the rite's starting point.

PREPARATION
The leader begins by reading these words from Lamentations, then sets the gathering in context.

> **Leader:** The steadfast love of the LORD never ceases,
>   his mercies never come to an end;
>   they are new very morning;
>   great is your faithfulness.
>   "The LORD is my portion," says my soul,
>   "therefore will I hope in him." (Lam. 3:22)

> **Leader:** Some circumstances of our lives press us so hard that we come to doubt ourselves or our own worth. We have gathered this day with [*Name*] as *he/she* struggles with [*Name and circumstance, such as being let go at work*] to stand with *him/her,* and to speak a word of encouragement from God.

The leader asks the participant to speak about what has happened. Together they write down a brief summary, just a sentence or two. [Example: There's a real problem here, and it's not of your making.]

OFFERING SUPPORT

Friends and family who are gathered are asked to speak about the circumstances in which their friend finds him or herself. If they agree with the summary, they sign their name on the paper under the summary. When all who want to have signed, the leader holds the paper, saying these words:

Leader: Keep these words in your heart, that the LORD is our God, the LORD alone. There is freedom and power in these words. No matter what the humiliation at someone else's hand, he or she is not God, and does not hold ultimate power over you.

(If the rite was preceded with confession and forgiveness, add these words:

Even if you have contributed to your own undoing, God is still your God, and ours is a God of new beginnings.)

Carry this paper with you. We hope that you will be encouraged by our signatures on this paper. Remember that we love you, and that God will sustain you. Let us pray.

Gracious God, you led Israel through the Red Sea and carried them safely to the other side. In Jesus, you calmed the storm on the sea. Be a strong presence now for [*Name*]. Bless this paper that *he/she* will carry with her as a sign of our love and support. Carry *him/her* through this time of difficulty; calm *his/her* anxious fears; and reassure *him/her* of your love for *him/her.* Into your hands we commend this dear friend, and all that is ours, trusting in your mercy through Jesus Christ, our Savior. **Amen.**

They conclude with a benediction:

Leader: The Lord bless you and keep you. The Lord's face shine upon you and be gracious to you. The Lord look upon you with favor and grant you peace. **Amen.**

Those gathered may continue their fellowship with a meal.

BLESSING A GAY UNION UNTIL THE
CHURCH IS READY TO BLESS

When you find someone to share your time
and you join your hearts as one,
I'll be there to make your verses rhyme
from dusk till rising sun.

John Ylvisaker[3]

In most Christian denominations today, there is no sanction for the blessing of same-sex unions. Some expressly prohibit them. Yet we no longer pretend there are no gay and lesbian people in our midst. In this interim time, while councils and denominations determine their next steps, gay and lesbian couples gather in alternate places, finding their own ways to bless their relationships. They take their hopes and dreams to their own ceremonies in parks and living rooms and backyards. While they wait for the church to be ready to bless their relationships, they work to imagine what that blessing should look like.

In 1986 our congregation decided to make a family pictorial directory. A photographer took pictures of all the households and prepared the directory. But while the photographs were being taken, an awkward moment occurred.

The directory company had a standard form that asked for the names of the people who would be in the picture, as well as addresses and phone numbers. Then participants were to mark the boxes that described the relationships of the people in the picture: husband and wife; mother/father and children; sisters and brothers. Larry and Roger didn't fit any of the categories.

I can no longer recall exactly how the conversation went: whether they told the photographer they were partners or just stood, waiting their turn. Whatever they said or didn't say, the photographer became flustered as he tried to complete their form. Annie stood nearby. An older woman in our church, she had volunteered to help get people ready for the photographer. Like many others in the congregation, she had never revealed her attitude towards the appearance of gay couples in our midst. Calmly, she turned to the photographer. It doesn't matter what the form says, she told him. They're family together. He left the boxes blank and took their picture, together.

Larry and Roger did not broadcast their status widely in the congregation—it was 1986, in church, and nobody did that then. Those who had eyes to see could see—they lived together, owned their home together, bought their cars together, were family together. But many were not ready to see. For Larry and

Roger, this tiny incident was a moving experience of belonging. Annie saw them for who they were, received them, honored their relationship with each other within our life together as a church. Because she chose to see and to make a place for them, they became less invisible.

A few years later, as our council discussed whether to publicize our welcome to Christians who are gay and lesbian, considerable apprehension was present around the council table. Some were afraid of being labeled a "gay church." One parishioner, Joyce, started us moving away from our fear. She talked about how being lesbian meant learning early on how to censor yourself, to hide part of yourself from others. In our church, no one before had ever spoken these words aloud in a public meeting. With courage she named herself. By doing so, she allowed the rest of the council both to name their fears and to acknowledge the welcome that already existed among us for gay and lesbian people. We all became less invisible.

Many couples come, starry-eyed, to prepare for their weddings believing that love will take care of everything. But that sentimental wisdom is just not true. When a couple matures in their relationship, when their love deepens and grows over time, when their marriage is sustained, yea, flourishes, it is not simply the partners' love that makes it happen. Their early affection for each other and their determination to make their relationship work count for something. But so do the many sustaining forces in family and community.

Like heterosexual couples, gay and lesbian couples need more than themselves to make their relationships flourish, more than their own household, when children come, to raise their children. In response to this need, in this ritual the arms of the participants, linked together, come to symbolize the strength of community in support of a couple. While they wait for the blessing of their church, arms raised together become the walls of the sanctuary in which the people become the signs of God's blessing.[4]

There is varied opinion about what should constitute a gay or lesbian commitment service. Is this a marriage? And should the service function like a marriage with language changes simply to acknowledge the gender of the participants? Or is it something else? As more lesbian and gay couples have public commitment ceremonies, a variety of ritual options will present themselves. This particular ritual, which consists of a series of community blessings, might be used as a simple ceremony by itself. Or it might be, as it was in the service for which it was created, the final portion—the prayers and blessings—of a gay wedding ceremony. The community blessings begin at the point in the service of the couple's promises and vows to each other, which are sealed with rings, the first circle of blessing.

What do I mean by blessing circles? A ring is one of the traditional symbols of marriage. Its circle is unbroken, a symbol both of God's love for the couple and the couple's love for each other, which, they hope and pray, will be sustained in their marriage until death parts them. In this ritual, participants gather in circles around the couple, link hands and raise them, as the pastor leads them through a series of spoken blessings of their relationship. Thus the ritual embodies layers of community support for a couple's relationship like the support that is taken for granted at a wedding ceremony in the church's sanctuary.

⌒⌒⌒⌒⌒⌒

BLESSING CIRCLES
for our children, especially for Kevin and Kate

This ritual originally took place outside. It was created for a couple whose church would not allow a ceremony for a gay couple to take place in the sanctuary. It may be held in any appropriate space that has an opening at the front or the center large enough for the participants to form circles around the couple.

During the ritual, participants are asked to assemble themselves in a series of different circles around the couple. The rite thus requires a strong leader who can speak with authority and offer clear directions. Rituals held outside often lack amplification. Leaders should prepare in advance by standing in the space where the service takes place: Is the space large enough to contain the number of participants expected, and for their safe movement as they are formed into circles?

Should a couple be permitted to hold their ceremony in a church's sanctuary, the Blessing Circles would still function to make visible the symbolic support of the community implied by a traditional wedding service—the blessings of parents, family, and friends, and of other couples, held within the walls of a sanctuary.

As in many weddings, there may be participants who are well suited to reading a lesson, leading a prayer, or otherwise exercising worship leadership.

Worship books regularly contain wedding vows. Many resources exist for working with couples to create vows. If the ritual is freestanding, work with the couple to prepare vows and insert them in the place noted below. If the rite is freestanding, the pastor opens with an invocation.

If the Blessing Circles are incorporated into a larger order of service, it begins with the exchange of rings.

When the leader first moves participants into circles around the couple, children eighteen and under form an inner circle around the couple and the remaining participants make an outer circle around the children. For a later blessing by committed couples, the leader asks couples to move into the inner circle and children and teens to move back to the outer circle. If there are only a handful of children, let them form a semicircle around the couple.

The leader should call out the blessings as a call and response, using short phrases that people can repeat back without hesitation.

The pastor begins with an invocation and continues with a prayer.

> **Leader:** In the name of the Holy One, who is our creator, and
> redeemer, and sustainer. **Amen.**
> O God, Author and Giver of life, Source of all that is good,
> visit us now, we ask you, that they who promise,
>   and we who bear witness to their hopes and bless them
> that together we may know Your power, O God,
>   and Your presence.
> We ask in Jesus' name. **Amen.**

The partners exchange vows with each other.

The pastor blesses the rings with this or similar prayer:

> **Leader:** We begin with two tiny circles, a sign of our hope for
> unbroken promises stretching forth from this day: "as long
> as they both shall live." The circle reminds us even more of
> your eternal love, O God, love that blesses us even when
> we falter. Bless these rings now, we ask you, and those who
> wear them. We ask in Jesus' name. **Amen.**

The partners exchange rings with these or similar words:

> **Couple:** [*Name*], this ring is a sign of my promises to you, of my
> love and my faithfulness.

The pastor concludes this portion of the service with a blessing using these or similar words:

> **Leader:** The eternal God be the foundation under your feet, to nur-

ture your love, that you might delight in each other until your life's end. **Amen.**

The worship leader introduces the community blessings with these or similar words:

Leader: You may know this couple differently than I do. But as I know them, this is a day and a service that belongs in church. I am not speaking about our hosts' hospitality when I say that this place does not seem quite right: their hospitality is gracious. Nor am I speaking of their yard; the setting is lovely. But knowing this couple, the most fitting place for this service would have been in church. They are leaders in the church. They worship each week in the sanctuary. But our church—our denomination—does not sanction such a service. (*If one of the couple is clergy, add:*) And our church does not allow its gay clergy any public option but celibacy.

Yet we know that part of what makes a committed relationship work is the institutional supports of community. Can you hear Luther Vandross singing, "Your love is all I need . . ."?[5] That's the sentiment of most love songs, but it's a lie! If we had to stand alone in twos, who could withstand the pressures of life?

In the next part of the service, we want to embody the support of our community for this couple in their committed life together. We will encircle them to bless them. (*Ask participants to form circles around the couple in the center of the yard: the couple in the center; children and teens up to age eighteen in a circle around them; everyone else around the children in another circle. The first three blessings, by family, friends, and children, take place in this first set of circles.*)

Leader: I'm going to lead you through a series of blessings and prayers as a kind of call and response. When I speak something, if these are words that you want to use for your blessing of [*Names*], say them after me. After the first two blessings, each time you speak a blessing, you will join hands with the people on either side of you. Don't worry; I'll lead you. Together you raise your hands like this in blessing. (*Have participants try linking hands and raising their hands together to be ready for the later section.*)

BLESSING CIRCLES

The pastor begins the blessings in this way:

Leader: Our arms—linked
our presence together
becomes the walls of sacred space
the sign of blessing
created here
NOW
for the time being
until the church is ready to bless.
By our blessings, we offer this relationship the support of the communities in which we
are rooted.

BLESSING BY FAMILY MEMBERS
The pastor leads family members with these or similar words:

Leader: We start with family members, wherever you stand in the circles. People come to a service like this expecting to hear vows. But there is something more. Families, you come to give your blessing. We come here today not just to make a couple but to bind two families to each other. I ask you, if you are here today as a relative of either of the couple, or if you were partnered into the family, would you consider speaking your blessing out loud?

Leader: We honor you as a new family

Family: We honor you as a new family

Leader: together.

Family: together.

Leader: I give you my blessing.

Family: I give you my blessing.

BLESSING BY FRIENDS

Leader: Friends, you play a different role: You know these two from the heart. Not by blood, but by choice, as friends can know. Friends come to bear witness. It is your role to hold on to the hopes and dreams that you feel in their presence today. There will be days when [*Name and Name*] do not remember their hopes and dreams. Then you will be there to remind them. You are a witness of the sweetness of their early love, of hopes unburdened by crisis.

Leader: We are witnesses to your love.

Friends: We are witnesses to your love.

Leader: I give you my blessing.

Friends: I give you my blessing.

Leader: Let us pray. Holy is your love, O God, and holy the love [*Name and Name*] have found in each other. Pour out your gifts, we pray, upon [*Name and Name*] in their life together: the Spirit of love, joy, peace, patience, kindness, generosity, faithfulness, gentleness, and self-control (Gal. 5:22). We ask in Jesus' name. **Amen.**

BLESSINGS BY THE CHILDREN AND TEENS IN THE FIRST CIRCLE

Leader: Children and teens, please join hands with the people on either side of you. Hold your hands up in the air and, if these are words you want as your blessings of [*Names*], say them after me: May your home always welcome children.

Children/Teens: May your home always welcome children.

Leader: We bless you.

Children/Teens: We bless you.

Leader: May you grow in patience with each other.

Children/Teens: May you grow in patience with each other.

Leader: We bless you.

Children/Teens: We bless you.

Leader: May your love deepen over time.

Children/Teens: May your love deepen over time.

Leader: We bless you.

Children/Teens: We bless you.

Leader: O God of wisdom and might, order our steps, that we might make space in our lives for those things that we do not easily do. May the fire of your love burn in us and lead us. **Amen.**

BLESSING BY ADULTS IN THE SECOND CIRCLE

Leader: Those of you in the second circle, would you join hands with the people on either side of you? Hold your hands up and, if these are words you want as your blessing of [*Names*], say them after me:

Leader: May the love of God shelter and protect you

People: May the love of God shelter and protect you

Leader: and those you love.

People: and those you love.

Leader: We bless you.

People: We bless you.

Leader: May your hearts be generous toward each other

People: May your hearts be generous toward each other

Leader: and toward others.

People: and toward others.

Leader: We bless you.

People: We bless you.

Leader: May your love, your home,

People: May your love, your home,

Leader: and your life together

People: and your life together

Leader: become a foundation stone of our community's life

People: become a foundation stone of our community's life

Leader: and of the life of the world.

People: and of the life of the world.

Leader: We bless you.

People: We bless you.

Leader: May you find strength

People: May you find strength

Leader: even in adversity.

People: even in adversity.

Leader: We bless you.

People: We bless you.

Leader: Let us pray. O God of our ancestors, we recall before you this day those dear to us who have gone on before us, naming them before you now in our hearts (*pause*). We bless you for their lives. Be with those who could not stand with us this day in the circles of blessing, for whatever keeps them from us. We ask your blessing on them. **Amen.**

BLESSING BY COUPLES
The leader asks the children and teens to move into the second circle and join

the adults. Then the leader asks all committed couples to move forward and form an inner circle where the children once stood. The partners face each other to receive a blessing. Holding hands, the "Marriage" couple raises their other hands and turns slowly as a couple as they speak this blessing on the other committed couples present:

Leader: Renew your bonds of love this day.

Couple: Renew your bonds of love this day.

Leader: We bless you.

Couple: We bless you.

Leader: May you be strengthened by God's presence

Couple: May you be strengthened by God's presence

Leader: and by the presence of this community with you.

Couple: and by the presence of this community with you.

Leader: We bless you.

Couple: We bless you.

Pastor: Let us pray. Gracious God, you give us each other, and provide the gifts of family and of community. Bless committed partners, husbands and wives, parents and children with your gracious presence to sustain them; we ask in Jesus' name. **Amen.**

BLESSING OF THE NEW COUPLE BY THE OTHER COUPLES PRESENT
The pastor asks the couples to face back toward the center of the circle and the "marriage" couple, then asks them to join hands with the people on either side of them, and to raise their hands in blessing.

Leader: Whatever comes, may you be faithful to each other.

Couples: Whatever comes, may you be faithful to each other.

Leader: We bless you.

Couples: We bless you.

Leader: May you dwell in God's presence.

Couples: May you dwell in God's presence.

Leader: We bless you.

Couples: We bless you.

Leader: Let us pray. Make of us, we pray you, O God, and make of these committed couples, building blocks of a strong community, foundation stones of a compassionate world. May they bear fruit that abides, we ask you in Jesus' name.

All: Amen.

BENEDICTION
The pastor concludes the service with a benediction.

Leader: May the Eternal God sustain you in love and in commitment, from this day forth, forevermore. **Amen.**

༄༅༅༅༅༅༅

BLESSING A DWELLING IN TIME OF ILLNESS OR ADVERSITY

Lord of all kindliness, Lord of all grace,
Your hands swift to welcome, your arms to embrace:
Be there at our homing, and give us, we pray,
Your love in our hearts, Lord, at the eve of the day.
                                              Jan Struther[6]

In a house blessing, participants normally walk through the rooms of a house or apartment. It is difficult to bless a nursing-home room as someone takes up residence there, if you have only an order for a house blessing to fall back on. Perhaps the person can no longer walk; the space that is now "hers" is less than one room. Just as her physical capabilities have diminished, so has the space that she now inhabits. There is no space that is hers alone. Whether she likes it or not, the most private parts of her life are now shared with others— her room, her bathroom, her visiting space. She can no longer care for herself. Many find it demoralizing or depressing to need so much care, to give up their freedom and independence, or to move from a loved home.

One of the main components of a house blessing is hope. It is hard to be hopeful, though, when one is facing a debilitating or incurable illness, or irreversible infirmity. Leading a "House Blessing" in such circumstances forces us to be honest. How can we, for instance, within the context of the ritual, assert a person's dignity, his or her worth before God, without becoming patronizing or condescending? (Recall the discussion in chapter 2 [p. 19] about how our bodies are used symbolically in worship.)

The following ritual asserts that our hope lies in God, and that God is present with us in both life and death. Thus participants may acknowledge real and costly losses, knowing God's ever-present support there, while at the same time also cherishing their earlier good health and former independence as gifts of God.

Traditional house blessings have a Scripture reading and prayer for each of the rooms. By walking through the rooms and reading and praying in each place, we are reminded that God's blessings exist for us in and through the physical surroundings of our home and the people with whom we share it. In contrast, the focus of this blessing for a nursing-home room shifts a bit. The room is still important as a place for God's blessing, but the starting point for the ritual becomes rather the relationship with God begun in baptism. The prayers for the new resident, for her family, for all who care for her, and for the nursing home all grow out of an affirmation of the covenant God began with us in baptism.

ᲝᲝᲝᲝᲝᲝᲝ

BLESSING OF A NURSING-HOME ROOM
in Memory of Irene

Continuing care options for the elderly currently provide such a range of options that a wide range of physical capabilities will be represented among those who move into such facilities, from independent living apartments through hospice care in a nursing home. Thus new residents' experiences will also vary widely, from relief at being able to give up the care of a home that had become unmanageable through despondency at leaving a beloved home. The following ritual was prepared for someone moving into a nursing home because of a significant physical decline and thus considers the blessing from that perspective. For someone with greater physical capabilities, worship leaders might compare a standard house blessing with the order offered here.

Discuss the possibility of a room blessing on an occasion before the event. The nursing-home resident will often be able to assist in planning this rite, at least in some basic ways. Does he have favorite hymns? Scripture passages? Who would she like to invite? What symbol of his or her earlier life might be blessed—a special piece of furniture? A lamp? Pictures of family? Or could there be some gift given and blessed as a sign of the past life that continues? In the following ritual, the African violet served that purpose, for Irene was a gardener. Even when she was confined to her apartment, she still surrounded herself with African violets.

Think about what symbolizes continuity and new life for the one with whom you will pray. Perhaps it is a sign of home or a gift related to the person's interests. Then rephrase the prayer of dedication (p. 51) to name the item and the way it shows forth the person's strength.

A new resident might welcome the opportunity to include in this rite moving around the nursing home for brief prayers—to the dining hall, solarium, or nurses' station, for example. Others, however, might find such a public procession embarrassing. As you plan the ritual, listen and you will be given clues to the shape of the blessing you do with this person. Some residents will prefer simple prayers led by the pastor in the room with no one else present.

In using or adapting this rite, you should be especially attentive to the awkwardness that some people may feel about praying in the presence of a roommate they do not know well. Should that other person be invited? Should the curtain be drawn? Who else might be invited? Family members? Someone from the nursing home? When possible, and if the new resident is open to it, consider bringing someone from the resident's home church to further demonstrate the bonds of Christian fellowship.

If your worship tradition does not use a creed in worship, you may substitute another kind of faith affirmation.

The service may conclude with Holy Communion.

You may need permission from a nurse or administrator to light a candle for this special occasion. The words may also be used without a candle.

AFFIRMATION OF BAPTISM
The leader begins with a confession of faith.

> **Leader:** A reading from the first letter of John: "Beloved, we are God's children now; what we will be has not yet been revealed. What we do know is this: when he is revealed, we will be like him, for we will see him as he is" (1 John 3:2).

Brother/sister in Christ: In Holy Baptism you were received into a covenant with God through which you also became a member of the Church. Through many and various changes in your life, you have been part of the community of God's people. As you settle now into this nursing home, we pause together that you might affirm your baptism in this time of transition. We ask God's blessings on you, on your new home, and on those who care for you.

I ask you now, [*with those who have gathered,*] to profess your faith, using the words of the Apostles' Creed.

All: **I believe in God, the Father Almighty,**
creator of heaven and earth.

I believe in Jesus Christ, God's only Son, our Lord,
who was conceived by the power of the Holy Spirit
and born of the virgin Mary;
who suffered under Pontius Pilate,
was crucified, died, and was buried;
who descended into hell.
On the third day he rose again.
He ascended into heaven,
and is seated at the right hand of the Father.
Jesus will come again to judge the living and the dead.

I believe in the Holy Spirit,
the holy catholic Church,
the communion of saints,
the forgiveness of sins,
the resurrection of the body,
and the life everlasting. Amen.[7]

Those gathered may sing a hymn or song.

HYMN SUGGESTIONS

"Come, My Way, My Truth, My Life"
"O God, Our Help in Ages Past"
"We Who Once Were Dead"
"Leaning on the Everlasting Arms"

The leader lights a candle, saying these words:

LEADER: "The LORD went in front of them in a pillar of cloud by day, to lead them along the way, and in a pillar of fire by night, to give them light" (Exod. 13:21).

Let us pray.

O God of Light, brighten this room by the light of your presence; we ask in Jesus' name. **Amen.**

Weather permitting, a window may be opened as a sign of the world outside. In colder weather, the drapes may be opened.

PRAYERS OF BLESSING
The leader leads participants through the following readings and prayers.

Leader: A reading from Paul's first letter to the Corinthians: "Love is patient; love is kind. . . . [Love] bears all things, believes all things, hopes all things, endures all things" (1 Cor. 13:4, 7).

Let us pray.

O God, give your blessing to those who share this room, that they may be blessed through their relationship with each other; that they may grow in patience, in kindness, and in hope. **Amen.**

Leader: A reading from the prophet Isaiah:
The LORD will guide you continually,
    and satisfy your needs in parched places,
    and make your bones strong;
and you shall be like a watered garden,
    like a spring of water,
    whose waters never fail. (Isa. 58:11)

Let us pray.

O God, most High, You sustain us and all living things.
Turn our hearts to You, that we may remember your mercy;
we ask in Jesus' name. **Amen.**

Leader: A reading from the Psalms:
It is in vain that you rise up early

and go late to rest,
eating the bread of anxious toil;
for [the LORD] gives sleep to his beloved. (Ps. 127:2)

Let us pray.

Father of mercy, God of love, let us rest in you; we ask in Jesus' name. **Amen.**

Leader: A reading from the prophet Isaiah:
Do not fear, for I have redeemed you;
I have called you by name, you are mine.
When you pass through the waters, I will be with you;
and through the rivers, they shall not overwhelm you;
when you walk through fire you shall not be burned,
and the flame shall not consume you.
For I am the LORD your God. (Isa. 43:1–3)

Let us pray for [*Name*] who takes up residence in this place.

O God of power and might, [*Name*] comes to this place because of changes in *her/his* body beyond *her/his* control. Support and uphold *her/him* in giving up *her/his* apartment/home in [*Name place*]. Give *her/him* patience through these days of transition and trust in your loving care, that whatever physical and mental changes may yet come, *she or he* may rest in the confidence of your loving care in the strength and dignity that belongs to all the children of God; through Jesus Christ our Savior. **Amen.**

Leader: Let us pray for the [*Name of the nursing home*].

Good and gracious God, you provide for our needs and surround us with hands that show forth your presence. We thank you for this place. We are grateful for [*Name of the nursing home*], for providing care that is not possible at home. We thank you for its gathering places that pull residents out of isolation. We remember before you now all who work here. By their skill and care make your love known. Give them kindness and compassion, patience and understanding. We ask in Jesus' name. **Amen.**

Leader: Let us pray for [*Name's*] family and friends.

God of mercy, we pray for [*Name the appropriate people*] and for all who will gather around [*Name*] in this place. Give them strength and hope, that family and friends may know themselves, together, as your children; we ask in Jesus' name. **Amen.**

Leader: A reading from Psalms:
> Thou, LORD, my allotted portion, thou my cup,
> Thou dost enlarge my boundaries. (16:5–6, *New English Bible*)

Let us pray.

Bless this [*Name item brought from home or church*], a sign among us of [*Name's*] life and strength. With it we celebrate how knowing [*Name*] enlarges us. We bless you, LORD, for *her/his* wondrous ability [*with plants*], for the work of *her/his* hands. May this [*African violet*] be a reminder to all who pass by of our love for *her/him;* we ask in Jesus' name. **Amen.**

The service may conclude with Holy Communion and with a final hymn or song, or may proceed directly to the benediction. In place of singing, participants may listen together to the tape of music from the home congregation.

HYMN SUGGESTIONS

"Amazing Grace"
"Beautiful Savior"
"I Love to Tell the Story"
"The Blood That Jesus Shed for Me"

Leader: The Lord bless you and keep you. The Lord's face shine upon you and be gracious to you. The Lord look upon you with favor and grant you peace. **Amen.**

MAKING THE THREADS OF COMMUNITY VISIBLE

I thank my God every time I remember you.
Phil. 1:3

Some would have called Robert dim-witted, but when he felt overwhelmed, he had enough wits about him to surround himself with his friends. Robert was mentally retarded; his ritual arose from him without conscious planning, like other examples of strange, patterned behavior in his life. Yet his impulse to surround himself with friends is helpful for us, especially when we think about people near us who have become isolated through difficult personal circumstances. To handle his fear when he was overwhelmed, Robert stopped where he was and stood still. He would start speaking quietly and raise his voice as he proceeded: he would call out the names of all of his friends, all that he could think of. By the end, he was actually shouting them out. It was a cathartic ritual, powerful enough to stand up to his fears.[8]

We can name the isolated people around us. Perhaps it is the person who has taken in an ailing aged parent; those who are trapped themselves by mental illness, or frailty or infirmity. The following rite was originally for the family of a chronically ill, disabled child whose medical condition isolated his family from their wider communities for months or years at a time.

As you consider this kind of ministry, take time to reflect on these questions: When? How? Who? What activities?

What might trigger celebrating this rite? **When** might it be appropriate? Discernment and sensitivity are required to answer this question. The right time is not usually in the midst of a crisis or hospitalization. Yet the weeks of recovery after a hospitalization or a flare-up might be. In your congregation, who notices when someone is missing from worship for a period of time? Is there an organization within your church that reaches out to the homebound? These existing groups may discover needs within the congregation before pastors or staff hear of them.

How might we approach such a ritual? While it is possible to conceive of celebrating this ritual for someone you do not know—a new neighbor, perhaps, who is caring for an aging parent—it is easier to imagine it strengthening and sustaining existing bonds of community. The fellowship meal below is set within the life of a congregation. It might be adapted for use by neighbors, friends, a book group, or a lunch group on the job. Family members who care for a disabled or infirm loved one usually continue to have some social connections, though they are less able to tend to them. Begin with the connections that exist.

Who should the visitors be? Invite people to take part who view the person with compassion rather than those who would attend out of obligation or pity. A person should not attend who has trouble looking at a child's crippled body, or who wants to turn his eyes from the chronic sadness in a parent's eyes. Those who attend should feel some connection with the family and be able to stand comfortably in the midst of sadness as well as joy.

Should other children be included? If the child himself is aware, or if there are other children in the household, discuss this with his parents. If children in the family feel embarrassed with other kids' "knowing," it is best to honor their wishes. On the other hand, if siblings in the family are open to it, this rite can be a wondrous gift, allowing other children in the family to connect with their peers who might see and better understand their family.

What activities, done together, might strengthen the connections between a disabled child and his family and their wider community? Begin by thinking about the community to which you and the family belong and things that can be visible in the community's public life: a Christmas ornament for the church's tree; bread baked for that week's communion; the week's flowers for the altar or other special occasion, arranged together. Let the project be something that the members of the family can do together and that they enjoy. Otherwise the attempt at reciprocity will not ring true. Consider the talents, interests, and abilities of the family; the season of the year; and the practices of the congregation or other group itself.

❦❦❦❦❦❦❦

FELLOWSHIP MEAL WITH THE FAMILY
OF A CHRONICALLY ILL OR DISABLED CHILD*
with Kathleen Hoye Powell
for Abby

Advance preparation will be necessary for this ritual. Plan ahead by setting a date with the family. Share with them the details of what you'd like to do with them, including bringing a meal that you all share together and an activity that you will have prepared but that you hope all of you can do together. Think carefully what you will need to bring with you to serve the meal. Before you arrive, speak with the family about what kind of space will be available, both for the meal and for the activity. Ask where to keep the food for the meal

*Janet S. Peterman and Kathleen Hoye Powell © 2001.

and where in the house you might all work on the activity together. Offer to stay after the meal to clean up. If the space will be limited in the family's home, plan accordingly about how many people should come along to participate.

The activity itself should probably take about half an hour, less if young children are involved. Think out the steps involved in the activity in advance and bring all of the necessary supplies with you. Planning is really important in this kind of ritual.

Check again on the day of the meal to be sure that the day is still OK.

SHARED ACTIVITY
As all are gathered in the area where you will work on the activity:

> **Visitor:** We have come to share this time with you, that the ties of our community life may be strengthened even now, while you are isolated by (*Name the circumstance directly, as for example, "Josh's condition, which requires that one of you always be home with him"*).

There will probably be time for conversation during work on the planned activity. Be sensitive not to pry, but visitors should provide some openings in the conversation to let the family know that they would like to hear about their experiences, as it seems appropriate. (Example: How is Josh recovering from his recent surgery? Will he be able to resume physical therapy soon?)

When the activity is complete, speak about how the project worked on together will become a sign of this family's life as a part of the wider community you share, using words like these: "When we use this bread in Sunday's communion service, we will include an announcement in the bulletin that we have prepared it together, as well as a special prayer for Josh and for your family in the church's prayers that day."

If the family wishes, they might lead the group in table grace as the meal begins. Or you may offer brief devotions according to the season and the practices of your community. The group may sing a Christmas carol or other simple song; someone may offer prayer or a brief Scripture reading.

SUGGESTIONS FOR SCRIPTURE READINGS: Ps. 121; Phil. 1:3–5; Heb. 11:1–3; John 6:1–14.

Toward the close of the meal, ask if there is anything the family needs that the wider community may be able to provide. Do not make promises you can-

not keep, but listen carefully to discern whether there are other ministries your congregation regularly offers that might be a help to them. (Examples: Meals? Respite care for a few hours?)

Ask if you may close with prayer. Be sensitive to the time available, to the physical needs of the one who is ill, and to the needs of small children. The ending prayers can be very brief, if necessary. Where possible, allow each person present either to add a petition to the prayer, or to voice concerns or thoughts that the one leading the prayer incorporates. A prayer litany in which all might participate could look like this:

> **Leader:** We'll close our time together now with prayer. I'll lead us with two sets of petitions. First we will name those things for which we feel grateful this day. You don't need to go around the circle, but each one may speak as he or she wishes. After each one speaks, we will all respond, "Thank you, Jesus." *(After the first petition[s] offered by those leading, leave ample time for others to speak. If often takes more time than you anticipate; wait patiently.)*

After all who want to have spoken, the leader leads the second prayer:

> **Leader:** We now place into God's hands those things that are difficult for us, for which we need guidance. As each one speaks, we will all respond, "Hear us, Lord." *(The leader models a prayer to start, like this: "We ask for rest, O God, for an uninterrupted night's sleep." After all have finished, the leader leads the group together in the Lord's Prayer: "Our Father . . . Amen.")*

✂✂✂✂✂✂✂

FOR FURTHER READING

Henri J. M. Nouwen. *With Open Hands*. Notre Dame, IN: Ave Maria Press, 1972, 1994, 1999.

Spencer Perkins and Chris Rice. *More Than Equals: Racial Healing for the Sake of the Gospel*. Downers Grove, IL: InterVarsity Press, 1993.

Renita J. Weems. *Just a Sister Away: Understanding the Timeless Connection between Women of Today and Women in the Bible*. New York: Warner Books, 1988, 2005.

Around Issues of Homosexuality

Audre Lourd. *Sister Outsider*. Trumansburg, NY: Crossing Press, 1984.

Melanie A. May. *A Body Knows: A Theopoetics of Death and Resurrection*. New York: Continuum, 1995.

Donnie McClurkin. *Eternal Victim, Eternal Victor*. Lanham, MD: Pneuma Life Publishing, 2001.

Jack Rogers. *Jesus, the Bible, and Homosexuality: Explode the Myths, Heal the Church*. Louisville, KY: Westminster John Knox Press, 2006.

Gretchen A. Stiers. *From This Day Forward: Commitment, Marriage and Family in Lesbian and Gay Relationships*. New York: St. Martin's Griffin, 1999.

Parenting and Children with Special Needs

Martha Beck. *Expecting Adam: A True Story of Birth, Rebirth, and Everyday Magic*. New York: Berkeley Books (Penguin Putnam Inc.), 1999.

Kathleen Deyer Bolduc. *His Name Is Joel: Searching for God in a Son's Disability*. Louisville, KY: Bridge Resources, 1999.

Rabbi Nancy Fuchs. *Parenting as a Spiritual Journey*. San Francisco: Harper Collins, 1996.

Henri J. Nouwen. *Turn My Mourning into Dancing: Finding Hope in Hard Times*. Nashville: W Publishing Group (Thomas Nelson, Inc.), 2001.

Chapter 4

Making Holy What Has Been Violated

Injustice anywhere is a threat to justice everywhere. We are caught in an inescapable network of mutuality, tied in a single garment of destiny. Whatever affects one directly affects all indirectly.
                                                                        Martin Luther King Jr.[1]

Sometimes in witnessing desperate trouble, I am startled not by the desperation but rather by the mercy and strength some discover in the cross of Jesus and the support they sometimes find in our congregation, like invisible lifelines. Is your congregation a place where people can come for a lifeline? Does your congregation's ministry reach out into your community with signs of compassion and healing?

Some people will not buy a house where a fire has occurred, even if the building has been completely refurbished. Some will not walk into a room where someone has died. Certain life experiences make us shudder. News reports invite us to gawk at violence, yet, up close, many of us turn away from people who have been hurt by violence.

The rites in this chapter respond to violent crimes—murder, suicide, and sexual violation, subjects often taboo in church. If these topics are taboo, how can a pastor venture where he or she has never been before, where few guides are willing to lead the way on the journey? Worship books rarely mention these horrible experiences. I was drawn to these places by listening to people in my church and neighborhood who had violence thrust upon them. As a child, one man was sexually abused for years by an older brother. He wanted to talk about why he kept forming such lousy intimate relationships. A woman's son was gunned down, caught in drug violence. I already knew these people, and I did not want to turn away. As I listened to them, in my other ear I heard hymns and Scripture verses offered to them for their healing.

Being on the street together where the woman's son was killed, washing his blood off the street, watching her begin to take leadership in our community to push back against the violence—these have felt like resurrection moments. Jesus was hanged on the outskirts of a city, at Golgotha, "the place of the skull," where common criminals were put to death. Yet Scripture tells us that God did not leave him there. When God raised Jesus, all those desolate places of human experience were brought with Jesus to the very heart of God.

In a ministry of worship and of presence, we are not asked to do what we cannot do. We are asked simply to follow where our listening takes us, to imagine the compassion of Jesus reaching out from the cross, through us. There, in the listening place, we will discover our own witness. Jesus beckons us to provide a space in which it is safe for victims of violence to find their own voices and to speak. Jesus invites us to become leaders who will listen and then speak a word from God. Our listening, our words, and our actions are invisible lifelines, drawing victims' attention to Jesus' wide open arms of healing.

MAKING HOLY WHAT HAS BEEN DESECRATED BY VIOLENCE

And the LORD said [to Cain], "What have you done?
Listen; your brother's blood is crying out to me from the ground!"
Gen. 4:10

Priestly and prophetic writing in the Old Testament make much of restoring property that has been taken unfairly. But how can we restore a sense of well-being when violence has shattered it?

In February 1992, Pia was struggling to break up with her boyfriend. She had told her father that she was afraid of him. Still, everyone was shocked when her boyfriend confronted her in the parking lot as she left work and after a brief struggle murdered her. The violence shook the hospital where she worked. Long after the blood was washed away, their shared experience of violence left many traumatized.

The impetus for this ritual came from Marguerite Sexton, a laywoman on the liturgy team of the Roman Catholic parish near the hospital. Pia's father was a member of the parish. After Pia's funeral, when Sexton listened to voices in the wider community, she understood that the woman's funeral had answered only some of their needs. Many at the hospital didn't know Pia well enough to attend the funeral, but they were still disturbed. Everyone found it hard to walk past that place in the parking lot where she had been killed. Sexton wanted believers to reclaim that place for life. She could visualize a ritual of blessing at the site where Pia was murdered. She wanted to be at the place with others. She also wanted to help the community take one little step back into life.

Worship books occasionally include prayers for victims of violence or for their loved ones, but they rarely incorporate the wider community. The scene of a murder or other violent crime is not simply an extension of the one who died, not, in this case, Pia's memorial. Her blood cried out for justice, but the ground where the blood was shed also cried out to be reclaimed for the sake of the ongoing life of the community.

This ritual took place on the grounds of the hospital. Sexton intended it for hospital employees, for community residents, and for Pia's family. Together they invoked God to take back what violence had desecrated—the site and the life of the community of people who use that place. A hospital official spoke; a priest from the parish was one of the prayer leaders. In other circumstances, lay leaders, deacons, or others who assist in the worship life of a congregation could lead such a ritual.

Like anyone who prepares a new rite, Marguerite Sexton made decisions along the way. For example, she knew that the wider pool of hospital employees included many who were not active participants in Christian churches. She wanted the rite to be as inclusive as possible for all the employees who wanted to come. Thus she chose to downplay specifically Christian references. She chose no Scripture readings. She made no explicit mention of exorcism, though she had in mind New Testament exorcisms like Mark 1:23–27 as she was creating the rite. She used aspersions, sprinkling water on a gathered people in remembrance of baptism, without explicit baptismal language.

The grief of the people gathered was so raw that Sexton chose not to give people the opportunity to speak. She decided that in not offering them the choice of whether to speak, she would relieve them of the obligation of speaking. She wanted to provide them with the greatest possible comfort. Their participation included encircling the spot and lifting their hands in blessing.

When Faye Dawson used this ritual to reclaim the street corner where her son Vincent was murdered, she felt it essential that the ritual be a Christian witness. With her pastors, she chose Scripture readings and prayers to add to the basic rite Sexton prepared. She also wanted parents of other murder victims to be able to speak if they desired it. She asked one parent to read the names of young people killed during the past year in their section of the city and another parent to offer words of encouragement.

Notice that in each case worship leaders worked with victims' needs as they understood them and as the victims could articulate them. People can react quite differently to the same set of circumstances. This core remained constant in both uses: gathering at the spot, reciting the Litany of Reclamation, and using hands and water to bless the place where blood was spilled. These sections were variable: whether to have victims speak; whether to read lessons from the Bible; and whether to light candles, like a vigil.

The passage of time changes what people need. The original rite took place soon after the murder. Dawson gathered people at the murder site nearly three months later. Sexton's original rite is printed below, noting where other sections, like Scripture readings, might be inserted.

᠎᠎᠎᠎᠎᠎᠎

BLESSING RITUAL: RECLAIMING A PLACE OF VIOLENCE*
by Marguerite H. Sexton

Unless holding a ritual on a public street involves a large crowd or blocks a major thoroughfare, securing municipal approval is usually not required. Institutional permission is often necessary to conduct a ritual on property that belongs to a hospital, business, or other public institution. If in doubt, inquire in advance.

Family members of victims of violent crime or others in the community often feel such desperate need to gather at the site of the crime that driving rain or bitter cold will not deter them. Discuss the possibility of inclement weather with core participants and decide ahead of time what might cause a postponement.

The leaders themselves may speak words of welcome to open the ritual or may invite someone else to bring the welcome—for example, a hospital administrator when the hospital owns the parking lot where a murder occurred.

If the family wants the group's presence at the site of violence to be a kind of antiviolence vigil, individuals may be given small candles as they arrive. Light the candles from one person to the next around the circle before begin-

*Marguerite H. Sexton © 1993. *Journeys of the Heart,* 547 Gibson Ave., Jenkintown, PA 19046.

ning the Litany of Reclamation. They remain lighted through the end of the rite. Participants then use one hand instead of two as they reach out their hands in blessing.

GATHERING
All present stand in a circle around the site of the violence. Prayer leaders welcome participants and gather them with a song and a prayer:

SONG: "KUMBAYA"

> Someone's weeping . . .
> Someone's praying . . .
> Someone's hoping . . .

Leader #2: God of life and hope, we call upon you now in [*name particular circumstance/time and place of the gathering: for instance, "this time of our anguish at Pia's murder as we stand where her life was taken from her"*]. We are in need of your mercy and your creative love. Help us to remember that in your name, all things are possible.

A leader may read one or more passages from Scripture.

SUGGESTIONS FOR SCRIPTURE READINGS: Pss. 6:1–3; 22:1–2; 55:1, 5–9; 88:1, 3 [psalms of lament]; Gen. 4:10; Jer. 31:15; Ezek. 45:9a-b [words about violence]; Gen. 28:16; Isa. 65:17–22; Jer. 31:2; Mark 6:7; Eph. 6:10–18; 1 Thess. 4:13–14 [words of encouragement].

WORDS OF ENCOURAGEMENT
A leader may ask someone to bring words of encouragement or may offer participants the opportunity to speak.

LITANY OF RECLAMATION
Prayer leaders lead the Litany of Reclamation that follows.

Leader #1: In God's name

Leader #2: Love overcomes hate
Peace overcomes war
Life overcomes death
Happiness overcomes sadness

Leader #1: In God's name

Leader #2: Good overcomes evil
Nonviolence overcomes violence
Freedom overcomes addiction
Generosity overcomes selfishness

Leader #1: In God's name

Leader #2: Healing overcomes pain
Mercy overcomes sinfulness
Comfort overcomes grief
Security overcomes fear

Leader #1: In God's name

Leader #2: Light overcomes darkness
Unity overcomes divisiveness
Hope overcomes despair
Laughter overcomes tears

At the Litany's conclusion, the prayer leaders bless the site of the violence by inviting participants to lift their hands and extend them toward or over the spot. Participants join the blessing action as they feel comfortable doing so.

Leader #1: Good and gracious God, let us forever be witnesses to the power of your saving grace. We thank you for the time we have spent at this place in safety and in comfort. Source of all life, you created us to be one with each other and with you. May the legacy of this terrible act of violence against our [*sister/brother*] mean a new resolve within each of us. Help us to be truly sisters and brothers to one another, treating all we meet with the respect and dignity deserving of the children of God. As partners with you, we are cocreators of life. This is our world, our earth, our sacred home.

We bless this place now. We claim it again for life and laughter. We consecrate it once again to you.

A leader dips an evergreen branch in water and sprinkles it on the gathered participants until the water has been sprinkled on all present. Then a leader pours the remaining water onto the ground they are blessing.

Leader #1: God our creator, in the very beginning you breathed upon the water, blessing it forever with your life force. May this sprinkling of water mark the beginning of new life for this place, made sacred by those of us gathered here now to claim it anew.

Those gathered may conclude with singing.

HYMN SUGGESTIONS

"Amazing Grace"
"This Little Light of Mine"
"Spirit of the Living God"
"Thy Word Is a Lamp"
"I Shall Not Be Moved"

BENEDICTION

Leader #1: May the God of life embrace us all. Go in peace to love and serve each other.

🙟🙟🙟🙟🙟🙟🙟

COPING WITH THE HOLIDAYS
AFTER VIOLENT CRIME

A voice is heard in Ramah,
   lamentation and bitter weeping.
Rachel is weeping for her children;
   she refuses to be comforted for her children,
   because they are no more.
                                  Jer. 31:15

More than a dozen years have passed, but some circumstances carry Sharon right back to the most difficult memories. She has sought support for herself in her grief and now works to support others in theirs. She has come a long way in her healing. But most years, still, she feels physically unwell from the early fall, the anniversary of her son's violent death, until the New Year arrives. Near this year's anniversary of his death, almost coincidentally, she heard that his killer was coming up for parole. For weeks she relived the trauma of his murder.

Grief of this sort often marks the parents, siblings, and other loved ones of murder victims for the rest of their lives. What can aid healing? What can allow them to move on, even to rededicate their lives, with the marks of grief shaping them in new ways? Such grief can last so long that survivors learn to censor themselves. They stop sharing their pain, sure that people won't want to hear—again—about the grief that will not go away. And it often happens that those close to survivors find it hard to know what to say or how to be supportive. Many withdraw in silence. Survivors often feel quite isolated, like no one is listening to them, and sometimes they are right. But that is not always the case.

In the crisis that ensues after a violent crime, new friends often rise up, or acquaintances draw near to become friends as others fall away. That shift, and survivors' vulnerability and great need, often opens up a rich opportunity for a congregation's ministry. In our congregation, when Faye's son was killed, women in the congregation who are part of a knitting ministry placed a knitted prayer shawl around her during the congregation's prayers one Sunday. Warm and thick, stitched with love and prayer, the shawl is a physical reminder that God is listening, even when it feels like no one else is. Grounded in that love, Faye was able to ask members of the congregation to support her as her son's killer went to trial.

Sharon McClain-Boyer found this kind of support in her church. Remembering how hard it was for her to get through the Christmas holidays without her son, one year she asked her pastor to help her lead an evening gathering for herself and for others whose loved ones were murdered. The gathering ritual she led has four parts: (1) introduction with a sharing of the stories of those who have gathered; (2) a discussion of grief with a minister or an experienced grief counselor; (3) a group discussion of strategies for coping with the holidays that calls on the wisdom and experiences of the attendees; and (4) a closing segment that uses candle lighting, notes to the ones who have died, and prayers and readings to lead people toward rediscovering peace and hope. Because this ritual is set within a larger church and community support-group gathering, it illustrates how a worship experience may focus and enhance ministries of outreach and pastoral care, especially among those who have no church affiliation.

Gathering survivors together also helps to rebuild communities shattered by violent crime. In large cities, murder and violent crime cycle in waves as gang and drug violence escalate and are then addressed more forcefully by communities and the police. Even one homicide tears at the fabric of community life; when violent crime becomes epidemic, the very core of community life is threatened. When your congregation gathers together those who suffer this kind of grievous loss, you help individuals and families as well as the communities to which they belong. Hearts torn by violence and grief will begin to carry the seeds of healing within them. And the bonds of healing shared among survivors will strengthen relationships, the building blocks of community life. This is true whether or not the people gathered become active in your ministry.

ᏃᏃᏃᏃᏃᏃᏃ

GRIEF SUPPORT GATHERING
FOR HOMICIDE SURVIVORS*
by Sharon McClain-Boyer
offered in gratitude for the life of Kevin
1970–1990

Set a date for this gathering at least a few weeks before the holiday. Those who are grieving will be anticipating the difficulty of the holidays before they can say it out loud. This gathering will help them find support throughout the holiday season.

A holiday gathering requires more advance planning than many others, for the potential participants tend to be isolated and invisible to the wider community. Many suffer alone. Gathering a large number of participants is not essential. Pastors, worship leaders, or those in outreach ministries can plan for this event with a few others, knowing that it can be beneficial for them even if only a few people attend. When you are responding to the needs of survivors that you know, their sense of what would be helpful can guide your planning. Or consider offering to help plan an event with grief support groups in your area, like Parents of Murdered Children. Then publicize the invitation where others can see it: in the local paper; at the library; at neighboring hospitals and churches; on the grocery store bulletin board. Provide contact telephone numbers (see the press release on pp. 72–73).

If you are planning the gathering with someone who has experienced the violent death of a loved one, ask if he or she would be willing to read the poem "Homicide" toward the end of the gathering. If that will not work, have

*Sharon McClain-Boyer © 1993. SharonWillie@aol.com.

the leader or other representative from the church be prepared to read it. If possible, talk with two or three participants in advance to see if they would be willing to share some of their experiences of grief when the discussion of grief begins.

Many survivors will find a church's sponsorship of the gathering and the presence of a pastor comforting and much needed for their own healing. Other survivors will still be searching for answers to relieve their anguish. Holding the gathering in a social hall instead of the main sanctuary may make the invitation feel more inclusive, or you might choose to hold it outside of a church building altogether. The meeting place should be easy to find, well lighted, and accessible.

The room should be set up before people arrive: a circle of chairs around a table with a large candle in the center. Alternatively, you may place the candle on a stand near the front of the room with chairs in a semicircle around it. If your church uses a paschal candle, it will serve well as the central candle. You will also need notepaper, envelopes, and a basket to hold them; two smaller candles for each participant; and some kind of tray or votive candle holders in which to place lighted candles.

At least one of the leaders should be warm and outgoing, greeting people as they arrive, introducing them to others who have already come. It is helpful to provide light refreshments as people arrive and also to have enough for the sharing of refreshments after the gathering.

OPENING
When the group has gathered, the leader briefly acknowledges the occasion for coming together.

> **Leader:** We have come tonight to find strength in being together. After the violent losses we have experienced, it is too hard to face the holidays alone.

Have one of the planners or a representative from the church read a selection from Scripture while the leader lights the central candle. Appropriate passages include Ps. 6:2–6; 13; 22:1–5, 14–21; Jer. 31:15; Luke 2:33–35 [words of grief and crying out to God].

SHARING STORIES
The leader opens group sharing with an invitation.

> **Leader:** As you are ready to share, name your loved one who was killed by violence. Tell us *his/her* birth date and

date of death. Share a memory of your loved one that sustains you.

As each one finishes sharing, he or she lights a small candle in memory of her/his loved one and sets it near the larger central candle. Even those who prefer not to share should be invited to light a candle. These candles remain lighted for the remainder of the gathering. When all have shared who want to share, a leader offers prayer.

Leader: Gracious God, with these memories of our loved ones you remind us of the joy and wonder of their lives. We thank you and praise you, heavenly Father, for the gift of their lives, even as we grieve, still, their passing. Surround and uphold us as we continue our walk through the valley of the shadow of death. We ask in Jesus' name.

All: Amen.

A hymn or song may close this portion of the ritual.

HYMN SUGGESTIONS

"Nobody Knows the Trouble I've Seen"
"Come, Ye Disconsolate"
"Precious Lord, Take My Hand"
"When Jesus Wept"
"Comfort, Comfort Now My People"
"O God, Our Help in Ages Past"
"Jesus, Savior, Pilot Me"

DISCUSSION: ACKNOWLEDGING THE REALITY OF GRIEF
A counselor, minister, or other leader speaks briefly about the different stages of grief and how family members deal differently with grief. Those present share their experiences as the leader guides the discussion using the suggested questions below.

Leader: Since Elisabeth Kübler Ross began her groundbreaking work on death and dying in the late 1960s, many have found it helpful to think of the experience of grieving as varied and moving through stages. Listen, for example, to Edward Wimberly's description: "Normal grieving is characterized by three phases. First, the grief sufferers yearn for the lost loved ones and experience anger toward the loved ones for abandoning them. The second phase begins when the bereaved accept the fact that neither yearning nor anger will bring the loved ones back. This leads to despair and disorganization in the lives of the bereaved. Following this phase is a period of reorganization, in which the bereaved turn toward the world and begin to find new relationships and meaning in life. During this period, the grief sufferers either begin the task of revising and editing the old story or begin to develop a new story without the deceased."[2]

Let's take a few moments to share our experiences with each other, as you want to share. (*Those approached in advance begin the sharing. Allow time for questions and sharing from the group.*)

1. Even though grief usually moves toward healing, often moving through recognizable stages, it isn't linear. It circles back around and often feels like it will never end. Where are you today in your grieving?

2. Sudden and traumatic death intensifies the experience of grief. Are there places where you feel stuck in your grieving? Or where the burden feels impossible?

3. Close family members don't all grieve in the same ways. Some are quiet about their grief, for instance, while others talk about it every day. Take a quiet moment to ask for the strength to accept and respect the journey of grief that each one is taking.

DISCUSSION: STRATEGIES FOR COPING WITH THE HOLIDAYS WHEN A LOVED ONE IS GONE
Using this or other resources, the leader gives examples of some activities that people have found helpful in previous years, then encourages participants to share their experiences with each other.

HOLIDAY ACTIVITIES CHECKLIST

Leader: I'm sure that you've shared many happy holidays with your loved one before your loss. Take a few moments to call to mind the last holiday you shared before he or she died. What was special about the holiday with your loved one? What is especially hard about imagining the holiday without him or her? Fill out the checklist you've been given (*distribute copies of chart on p. 70*). Use the blank spaces to fill in activities of your family not already listed.

When the group has had enough time to work on the checklist, have group members share with the group, as they wish to, an activity that they will find especially painful about the coming holiday without their loved one.

Leader: Share with the group one holiday tradition in your family that will continue even without your loved one.

So much about this holiday has changed by your loved one's death. Are there ways you can imagine appreciating starting some new holiday traditions this year? (*Let the group share and discuss, including ideas from group members whose loss is not so recent. If they have a hard time getting started, have some suggestions ready. Examples: Find a way to take a holiday meal to someone who is homebound. Buy toys in memory of your loved one for needy children.*)

FINDING PEACE AND HOPE THROUGH GOD
Provide each participant with a small candle and a note card and envelope. Introduce a few moments of silence with this instruction.

Leader: One of the hardest things about losing a child or sibling, parent or partner suddenly and tragically is that loved ones often feel that they have unfinished business with the one who has died. If you would like, you may write a note to your loved one and seal it in the envelope, to offer it here in this basket to your loved one. You may wish to write a message especially tied to these holidays approaching or of something in your family's life. When you seal the envelope, you can know that your thoughts, your message, will be kept confidential.

Allow participants ten minutes to complete notes. Gather them in a basket and place the basket near the lighted candles on the table.

Holiday Activity Shared	Yes/No	Memory Associated with This Activity	Continue This Year? Or Avoid This Year?
Cook special foods			
Share special meal			
Decorate Christmas tree			
Buy gifts for the loved one			
Receive gifts from loved one			
Purchase Christmas tree			
Visit with relatives			
Attend Church			
Bake cookies			
Play games together			
Visit with friends			
Visit the cemetery			
Decorate house			

New activities I might like to try this holiday season . . .

Leader: Earlier we each lit a candle in memory of our loved ones whose lives were cut short by violence. Now we will each light a peace candle for ourselves as we pray for peace in our hearts. When you are ready, take your candle to the central candle, light it, and bring it back to your seat with you.

The leader pauses as participants begin to light their candles, then says:

LEADER: As you light your candle be reminded of the presence of God with us. When Jesus returned to his disciples after he died, he said to them, " 'Peace be with you. . . . Receive the Holy Spirit' " (John 20:21, 22). In his ministry, Jesus often spoke of peace: " 'Peace I leave with you; my peace I give to you. I do not give to you as the world gives. Do not let your hearts be troubled, and do not let them be afraid' " (John 14:27).

When all the candles are lighted, one of the event planners reads this poem.

HOMICIDE SURVIVORS

I have to become a survivor and I can do it.
The hardest part of my loss I have been through it.
Having to face this world again, I will learn to pretend
Until my broken heart has time to mend.

The grief and pain I'm feeling is my own
But it's easier knowing that I'm not alone.
Sadness, heartache, loneliness and pain
Tragic death is hardest on those who remain.

I have to become a survivor now and I can do it.
I'll ask God and He will help me get through it.
Sharon McClain-Boyer

The leader closes the gathering with a reading from Scripture, a hymn, and a benediction.

SUGGESTIONS FOR SCRIPTURE READINGS: Pss. 23; 139:7–12; Isa. 49:13–16; 60:18; Lam. 3:22–23; Matt. 5:4; John 11:32–35; 14:25–27; 2 Cor. 12:22–26, esp. v. 6; 2 Thess. 2:16–17; Rev. 21:1–5 [words of comfort and encouragement].

Hymn Suggestions

"The Lord Will Make a Way"
"Jesus, the Light of the World"
"Give Me Jesus"
"Balm in Gilead"
"When Peace, Like a River"
"The Blood That Jesus Shed for Me"
"His Eye Is on the Sparrow"

Leader: The Lord bless you and keep you.
The Lord's face shine on you and be gracious to you.
The Lord lift up his countenance upon you and give you peace.

All: Amen.

Participants are invited to remain for fellowship time with each other over the remaining refreshments. If it seems appropriate, provide some means for participants to share contact information with each other to encourage ongoing support.

⚶⚶⚶⚶⚶⚶⚶

SAMPLE PRESS RELEASE
SURVIVING THE HOLIDAYS AFTER VIOLENT DEATH

The holidays are a joyous time for many families. For some, however, holidays can be very sad and difficult, and these people wish they could just fly from Thanksgiving to New Year's and let the rest of the world celebrate without them. The aftermath of violence is devastating, and the holiday season is another obstacle to overcome. For all who have experienced the death of loved ones through acts of violence, difficult days lie ahead.

When we come together, though, we are given strength and sometimes even peace. Hear Sharon McClain-Boyer's invitation, one mother's witness:

PEACE
WELCOME
VIOLENCE has already taken its toll
We must try to put it on hold
Laughter, understanding, and love we'll share

You are among people who care.
No charge to join in
Please have no fear.
The precious price has been paid
by death, blood, and tears.
Though it should have never begun
The time has come for it to end.
PEACE

[Name of your church] *will offer a grief support gathering called* **Surviving the Holidays after a Loved One's Violent Death** *on* [date and time] *at* [location and address]. [Names of people who will lead, including title for pastor or other leader. Note that one of the leaders has experienced a similar loss, if appropriate.]

If you have lost a loved one to violent death, you are invited to gather with others who have experienced similar losses to find strength, encouragement, and hope. Recent survivors as well as those whose losses occurred in previous years are invited to attend. Youth and adults will have a special time for remembrance, will share stories, and discuss grief and strategies for coping with the holidays. The gathering will conclude with candle lighting, Scripture reading, and prayer. For more information, contact [Name and telephone number.]

ᙚᙚᙚᙚᙚ

USING RITUAL WITH THE BEREAVED
SURVIVORS OF SUICIDE
with Florence Gelo

There are some griefs so loud
They could bring down the sky,
And there are griefs so still
none knows how deep they lie . . .
May Sarton[3]

At important moments in the life cycle, rituals not only mark a change, they also effect change. Two lovers come to the altar and the marriage service weds them, makes them husband and wife. They leave the altar transformed. Among people who grieve violent deaths, or who need to heal from trauma, transformation is more incremental. Healing from grief is not a once-and-done experience. But neither is ritual's power in these circumstances inconsequential. Ritual contains within it the capacity to move participants toward wholeness and healing.

Where and how might bereaved survivors of suicide need to be moved? When Jeff took his life, his wife Lori found his body. Months and months later, it is not the image of the stool fallen over on the ground that she remembers, nor the full-length image of Jeff's body. What has colonized her dreams and intrudes unexpectedly, exhaustively, into the dreary hours of her day is the strange, odd, and unlikely image of Jeff's sneakers and khakis framed in her kitchen window.

Like others who witness trauma or the intense suffering of another, those whom suicide leaves behind are often haunted with an actual or imagined mental image. The emotional impact of suicide is devastating. More than 29,000 people in the United States die by suicide every year. Thousands of bereaved survivors are left shattered and plagued by grief and loss as they struggle to understand. Sudden or violent deaths intensify the experience of grief. In addition to grief's regular course, those left behind after a suicide often experience shame; stigma; isolation; a sense of abandonment; helplessness, which is often experienced as guilt for not having been able to prevent the suicide; despair; and the painful, urgent demands of unanswerable questions.

The bereaved often feel tremendous guilt, somehow believing that they should have known that their loved one was in danger or should have been able to prevent the act itself. Death of a loved one by suicide also adds to the survivors' isolation. Unlike natural death, suicide is often difficult to discuss, even with family and close friends. In their anguished question "Why?" many bereaved survivors are also asking, "Why, God, have you forsaken me?"

The ritual below aims to address these circumstances in the following ways: (1) Inviting others in a congregation who have also experienced trauma or difficulty to be present with them helps survivors see that they have a place among others who are suffering, easing both the isolation and the stigma associated with suicide. (2) Avoiding a rite of confession and forgiveness shifts the focus away from self-blame, where survivors often get stuck. The rite rather acknowledges the tragic reality that even with our best efforts we are often helpless to save our loved ones. Then it seeks the compassion of God for healing. (3) Emphasizing God's compassion offers a clear public statement that the church no longer teaches that suicide is an unpardonable sin.

The heart of this rite is twofold: it provides an occasion to remember the person's life, among others who are remembered; and, with a visualization meditation, it seeks to help transform a haunting visual image from a plaguing relived experience to a less painful memory. The visualization offers respite through mental images of beauty and tranquility, affirmations of life that can help survivors to rest from the weariness and stress of a single, horrible last image.

~~~~~~~~

HEALING SERVICE AFTER SUICIDE OR VIOLENT DEATH AND REMEMBRANCE OF LOVED ONES WHO HAVE DIED*
by Florence Gelo

When the news of a suicide first reaches a congregation, let there be a prayer in public worship for the one who has committed suicide and for his/her family. With such a prayer, leaders set the tone for compassion rather than judgment.

Choose a time for this ritual in consultation with the survivors. The early months of grief are too soon, too raw; anniversaries of the suicide, too, are often too intense, even years later. Help the bereaved survivor find another appropriate date—perhaps a birthday, another anniversary, or the season of a person's favorite sport or other activity. These dates remind participants of the person's life, not the circumstances of his or her death. A date might also be appropriate at a moment in the flow of a congregation's regular worship life, near All Saints' Sunday, for example, or around the turn of the year.

This worship experience might work especially well in a small group or retreat setting. Allow enough space in the sanctuary, chapel, or other place so that participants need not be crowded too tightly together, yet not so much space that they are scattered as single individuals, far from each other.

If possible, plan this worship experience in consultation with bereaved survivors and/or others who might benefit from it. Then publicize it within the congregation and wider community with an invitation for any who feel wounded by life. Make mention of those who are left behind after suicide, but make the invitation broader so as not to isolate or further stigmatize.

Have others from the congregation present to lead the readings and

*Florence Gelo © 2004. 1505 Firethorne Lane, Wyndmoor, PA 19038.

perhaps also the singing and/or the prayers, thus extending the congregation's ministry in care and outreach. You will need a chime or something else that makes a gentle musical sound to end the visualization. Following the worship experience, extend the fellowship of healing with refreshments or a meal. As people gather, play music softly to set the tone.

Invite people into the purpose of the service.

> **Leader:** We gather this day struggling with difficulties that are hard to put into words. Many of us feel wounded by life or by a traumatic experience. We gather this day to seek the healing and comfort of God and of each other.
>
> Let us pray.
>
> O Gracious God, Spirit of Life, whom we know as love and comfort,
> > at this difficult time, when our pain is felt so deeply,
> > and we feel so alone,
> > be with us and make your presence known.
>
> Let peace and quiet of mind come in the evening.
> Let an opening heart greet us in the morning.
> Help us find love and acceptance in the torrents of anger,
> > hope and vision in place of despair.
>
> Though we alone can find that silent place where healing begins,
> > lift our burdens, ease our fears, and grant us peace.

All: Amen.

The congregation sings the spiritual "Nobody Knows the Trouble I've Seen" or another appropriate hymn.

HYMN SUGGESTIONS

"Abide with Me"
"Jesus, Savior, Pilot Me"
"Over My Head"
"Precious Lord, Take My Hand"
"Though Gathered Here to Celebrate"

READINGS
A reader reads this poem, then one or more passages from Scripture.

Stars, Songs, Faces

Gather the stars if you wish it so.
Gather the songs and keep them.
Gather the faces of the women.
Gather for keeping years and years.
    And then . . .
Loosen your hands, let go and say good-by.
    Let the stars and the songs go.
    Let the faces and years go.
    Loosen your hands and say good-by.
                  Carl Sandburg[4]

SUGGESTIONS FOR SCRIPTURE READINGS: Pss. 6:1–7, esp. v. 6; 22:1–2; Eccl. 3:1–8; 8:4; Jer. 45:3; Mark 15:34 [grief]; Ps. 121; Jer. 29:11; Matt. 1:23; 11:28–30; John 14:1–3; Rom. 5:1–5; 8:31–35, 37–39 [the comfort of God].

The leader directs a guided meditation.

Leader: Part of the process of healing involves creating positive new images that we can carry within us. I'd like now to suggest that you reflect on an image from a past experience . . . one that makes you feel peaceful. Settle down, sit comfortably, and relax your body. [*pause three seconds*] Let go of any tension you feel in your shoulders [*pause*], your arms [*pause*], uncross your legs [*pause*], and relax. If you like, close your eyes, and listen closely to my voice.

Imagine a place where you feel calm and serene, a place that is for you beauty without words. Select an image that makes you feel centered and peaceful. [*pause*]

Go to that place within, and rest there.

Hold the image in your mind—notice the details [*pause five seconds*]—the color [*pause five seconds*], sound [*pause five seconds*], and fragrance. [*pause a few seconds longer*]

Absorb the serenity into your body—let it fill you. [*pause ten seconds*]

When your mind wanders, notice what distracts you.

Let the image come back to you. [*pause five seconds*]

Look closely at the contents of your mind. [*pause five seconds*]

When your mind wanders again, gently return to this image—this place of calm—with each new breath.

Stay with this image. In a few minutes you will hear the sound of the chime that will invite you to open your eyes and, feeling calm, come back to the present moment.

[pause two or three minutes, then ring chime]

Leader: All of us have undesirable or uncomfortable thoughts and images that enter our minds. It is important to know that it is possible to gain control over them. We can practice distracting ourselves, or replacing these images with pleasant and positive ones—images more comfortable and healing. I invite you to make this visualization a daily practice, if possible. If a daily practice feels overwhelming, take a few minutes whenever you can to sit peacefully and quietly and turn your mind to positive thoughts and images.

Those gathered now take a moment to be silent—to move from quiet meditation to singing the next hymn. Play music softly in the background to lead up to the hymn.

HYMN SUGGESTIONS

"Nearer My God to Thee"
"Jesus Loves Me"
"O Love That Will Not Let Me Go"
"What Wondrous Love Is This"
"Bring, O Morn, Thy Music"
"I Cannot Think of Them as Dead"
"I Know This Rose Will Open"
"I've Got Peace like a River"
"Sovereign and Transforming Grace"

The leader leads the people in prayer.

Leader: Help me, God of Compassion, for I endlessly seek to understand the "why" of this mystery of death. As much as I desire to be whole once again, my pain is unceasing, heavy, and deep. I am bitter and angry, and my heart is sealed from hope. Spirit of Life, send relief from confusion, guilt, and despair. Support me. Guide me. Restore me. Heal me. Let me find a quiet peace that I may live fully once again.

All: May God's name be blessed forever.
May the One who creates harmony above and within
make peace for us and our loved ones
and let us say Amen.

Leader: Even as we pray for ourselves in our suffering, we pause also to pray for all who have taken their own lives. [*pause*] How we wish that it could have been otherwise! [*pause*] We give thanks for their lives. We give thanks that their pain has come to an end. [*pause*] Grant their loved ones, we pray, relief from anguish and despair. [*pause*]

We pray for those whose suffering, even now, feels interminable, for those who contemplate a violent or abrupt end to their misery. [*pause*] Spirit of Compassion, be a strong presence to all who suffer in this way still. [*pause*]

Silently and aloud, we name before you, O God, our loved ones who have died.

Keep silence while participants call out names.

Let us open now our hearts to grieve our losses, as we remember our loved ones.

LITANY OF REMEMBRANCE

Leader: At the rising of the sun and at its going down

All: We remember them.

Leader: At the blowing of the wind and the chill of winter

All: We remember them.

Leader: At the opening of the buds and in the rebirth of spring

All: We remember them.

Leader: At the blueness of the skies and in the warmth of summer

All: We remember them.

Leader: At the rustling of the leaves and in the beauty of autumn

All: We remember them.

Leader: At the beginning of the year and when it ends

All: We remember them.

Leader: As long as we live, they too will live;

All: for they are now a part of us, as we remember them.

Leader: When we are weary and in need of strength

All: We remember them.

Leader: When we are lost and sick at heart

All: We remember them.

Leader: When we have joy we crave to share

All: We remember them.

Leader: When we have decisions that are difficult to make

All: We remember them.

Leader: When we have achievements that are based on theirs

All: We remember them.

Leader: As long as we live, they too will live;

All: for they are now a part of us, as we remember them.

Rabbis Jack Riemer and Sylvan Kamens[5]

The service concludes with a sharing of the peace.

Leader: The peace of the Lord be with you always.

All: And also with you.

Those present are invited to share the peace of God with each other. When they have finished, the leader concludes with a benediction.

Leader: May you be comforted and strengthened. Go now in peace.

All: Amen.

ᖑᖑᖑᖑᖑᖑ

HEALING FROM SEXUAL ABUSE

As for me, where could I carry my shame?
Tamar, 2 Sam. 13:13

In my neighborhood, old iron fences mark the property lines around some neighbors' yards. The fences are very old. Over time, as trees nearby have grown, iron bars of the fence held unyielding in the earth have worked themselves into the trunks of some of the trees. What first stood near the tree, then rested against its bark, is now, many years later, deep in the flesh of the tree. The tree grows on, but at what cost to itself with an iron stake embedded in its flesh?

Sexual abuse is an abuse of power. Whether it takes place between adult and child, or boss and worker, or a relative or relative's partner and a teen in the home, these inappropriate boundary crossings are like the iron stakes. The original abuse is an experience of trauma, and often not a single occurrence. Silence and denial and the victim's shame cover over the trauma with many layers, grown over time. In all its perversion, it is still connected to the rest of the fence, rooted in the community's life.

What kinds of worship experiences might help someone heal from past sexual abuse? Often in the church, victims of sexual abuse encounter more silence and denial than welcome. Preaching, teaching, prayers, and congregational discussion rarely touch on the experience of abuse or point to its healing. Even the biblical stories that deal most directly with sexual abuse are almost never chosen for public reading.

In the three-year cycle of lectionary readings used by liturgical churches and others, for example, the following stories are completely absent. There are many readings from the patriarchal narratives in Genesis, but not the story where Lot offers his daughters to rapists (19:1–10). The rape of Princess Tamar is similarly passed over in silence (2 Sam. 13:1–22). So, too, does the lectionary skip the stories in Judges of the sacrifice of Jephthah's daughter, and the unnamed woman who was raped, killed, and dismembered (11:29–40; 19:1–30). Churches where preachers choose their own biblical texts are rarely different in this regard. The church's silence nearly shouts, "We don't talk about these things here!" Often victims take the silence more personally. Feeling their own shame, they hear the silence telling them, "You don't belong here."

For their healing, victims of sexual abuse need to find ways to peel back the layers of silence and denial. They need to be able to find their own stories, to speak them in their own voices, to ask for what they need.

Linda Hogan went home to her people for a sweat lodge ceremony. She was looking, she says, for renewal, for a "point of return." First she went to a deeply spiritual man, a leader of her Chickasaw people. She sat with him, ate with him, then she told him why she had come. Reflecting later on her experience with the sweat lodge ritual, Hogan says that story, that is, putting her story into language as she spoke to him, "is at the very crux of healing."[6]

The ritual below is designed for an individual's personal use, that in the words of others readers may begin to find their own voices. Pastors are often aware of people who are struggling with past abuse. If so, they could pass on the ritual to that person for a season of healing, perhaps corresponding to a season like Lent, or during the time of a church's revival. The readings can be a good complement to working on the issues in psychotherapy.

Many, however, are not yet ready to speak of their experiences to others, especially not in church. The congregation might print up copies of these readings and leave them in a public place for members to take for themselves. Many will prefer a private, personal way of using these resources. For those already in conversation about these things with others, there is an alternate use for the personal rite below, designed for a time with a minister or prayer partner.

When victims of sexual abuse have been sworn to secrecy, how shall they learn to speak of their own experiences? In the ritual below, psalms of lament give voice to a range of experiences and feelings common to those who have been abused: a sense of abandonment, despair, hope, a sense of uncleanness, a longing for healing and for God, isolation, fear, and strength. Woven through the readings that follow are writings from poet Trapeta Mayson and the words of two beloved spirituals and a hymn. With the words of others, abuse survivors can begin to strip away layers of denial and secrecy to find their own stories. In prayer and meditation, they begin to heal.

Within a congregation, leaders' conduct, whether overt and thoughtful or filled with denial and inaction, is still a primary factor for setting the tone. Does your congregation respond to those who have experienced sexual abuse as powerless victims? As people who got themselves into trouble? Or are they survivors searching for healing? When we find ways to speak openly in church of sexual abuse and of the possibilities for healing from its trauma, we offer the community's resources of comfort and healing to people who often feel isolated. This might be as simple as a general prayer in thanksgiving for those who are finding healing from past traumas or a brief note in the church's worship bulletin about the availability of personal worship resources for those who have experienced past sexual abuse.

Pastors and worship leaders need to tread lightly in their offers of support. Victims of sexual abuse often feel an intense unworthiness, deeply rooted shame, and resistance to participating in the life of a community. Perpetrators of the violence are often still nearby. How you handle touch is especially important. Because abuse is a boundary violation, people seeking healing from abuse often have difficulty finding appropriate touch; the boundary is often not clear to them. Taking the person's hand, touching an arm, or hugging often feel like unwelcome intrusions. In the alternate version of the rite below with a prayer leader, there is no laying on of hands, no kiss of peace. Some might request these things, which then opens a door for conversation. These ritual actions, however, are consciously omitted.

⌇⌇⌇⌇⌇⌇

MEDITATIONS FOR FINDING YOUR VOICE:
A DAILY RITUAL FOR THOSE WHO HAVE BEEN
SEXUALLY ABUSED
with Poetry by Trapeta B. Mayson*

The readings in this healing ritual are designed for meditation and reflection by someone who has experienced sexual abuse. Pastors may offer the ritual to congregants for their personal use. A simple prayer service that incorporates a daily reading of one of the texts below provides a form and setting for congregants' use.

When a person uses one reading per day, she or he may want to use them over the course of a month set apart for more intense prayer for healing. Some find it helpful to cut the readings apart to glue them onto the pages of the journal, leaving space for personal reflections on the meditations. Using such a journal encourages victims to put their own experiences into words, a practice that many victims of sexual abuse find healing. Setting apart a corner, perhaps with a candle or cross or other object of focus, often aids meditation.

Alternatively, pastors might use selections from the readings in a time set apart for prayer with a congregant. When a minister leads someone through a meditation time around these texts, pay special attention to the setting. The

*Poetry copyright © 2003 and 1997 by Trapeta B. Mayson. Used with permission. Trapeta@aol.com.

rite should take place in a physical setting, like a chapel or sanctuary, that is quiet, set apart from the daily press of activities, and completely free from intrusion or interruption.

ORDER OF DAILY PRAYER FOR PERSONAL USE

Choose a familiar hymn or song to begin the period of meditation. If you do not feel comfortable singing, play a selection on tape or CD to settle into the quiet time.

HYMN SUGGESTIONS

- "I Love the Lord, Who Heard My Cry"
- "When Jesus Wept"
- "Jesus, Savior, Pilot Me"
- "O Sacred Head Now Wounded"
- "In the Name of Jesus/Victory Is Mine"
- "Somebody Prayed for Me"
- "Blessing Our Names"

Blessing Our Names

9.9.9.4

Author Unknown

Bless this name: (name) Wak-en un-to God, you ho-ly ones.
(these) (names):

Let no more your bless - ing be un - sung. Let all peo-ple

know the Christ in you. Al - le - lu - ia.

READING

Working through the readings in order, the participant takes one reading from the meditation texts, poems, and spirituals below; reads it slowly; then keeps a time of silence reflecting on the reading. Do not move too quickly through the silence. The participant may take time for reflecting in a journal as part of the response to the reading and may close with prayer.

PRAYER

Spoken by the participant, silently or aloud:

> **Participant:** Eternal God, in whom we live and move and have our being: I praise you for the gift of life, for the gift of this day. Heal me, I ask you, and help me to find my own voice. I ask in Jesus' name. Amen.

ORDER FOR A TIME OF PRAYER TOGETHER

When using this prayer time with someone, prepare the space with a candle and comfortable seating. Be sure that others will not interrupt during the prayer time.

Before the prayer time, choose a series of four to six readings from the meditation texts, poems, and spirituals below that speak to the needs of the person asking for prayer, as you understand those needs.

Follow the order for personal prayer above with an opening hymn or music selection, readings, and prayer. The leader and participant may alternate reading the texts aloud, or the leader may read them all. Keep silence after each reading. Close with prayer:

> **Leader:** Gracious God, you are always more ready to hear our prayers than we are able to speak them. We pray for [*Name*]: In the sighs of *her/his* heart, let your Holy Spirit intercede on *her/his* behalf. Bring your healing. Bring your peace. We ask in Jesus' name. **Amen.**

MEDITATION TEXTS, POETRY, AND SPIRITUALS

> As a deer longs for flowing streams,
>   so my soul longs for you, O God.
> My soul thirsts for God,
>   for the living God.
> When shall I come and behold
>   the face of God?

My tears have been my food
   day and night,
while people say to me continually,
   "Where is your God?"
Ps. 42:1–3

It is not enemies who taunt me—
   I could bear that;
It is not adversaries who deal insolently with me—
   I could hide from them.
But it is you, my equal,
   my companion, my familiar friend,
with whom I kept pleasant company;
   we walked in the house of God with the throng.

And I say, "O that I had wings like a dove!
   I would fly away and be at rest."
Ps. 55:12–14, 6

Save me, O God,
   for the waters have come up to my neck.
I sink in deep mire,
   where there is no foothold;
I have come into deep waters,
   and the flood sweeps over me.
I am weary with my crying;
   my throat is parched.
My eyes grow dim
   with waiting for my God.
Ps. 69:1–3

Nobody knows the trouble I see,
Nobody knows my sorrow;
Nobody knows the trouble I see,
Glory, hallelujah!
Traditional Spiritual

For you are not a God who delights in wickedness.
Ps. 5:4

O LORD, why do you cast me off?
   Why do you hide your face from me?

Wretched and close to death from my youth up,
I suffer your terrors; I am desperate.

Ps. 88:14–15

Healing Song

There is a place where we go
to put our burdens down,
to unfold ourselves,
to detach from pain,
to gather loss,
to reconstruct,
to rebuild.

There is a place where we go,
and know that we are children of God,
he is in us,
his love covers wounds;
it is the needle, the thread
stitching us back together again.

And in that place
we wail to the creator,
we call on the ancestors
on bended knees,
hands raised,
hearts heavy,
spirits weakened,
we sing,

Oh Creator,
You who understand us,
You who know us,
You who love us,
Come Heal, Come Heal.

We sing,
Oh Creator,
we are seeking renewal,

we are seeking rebirth,
we are seeking you
Come Heal, Come Heal.

SiTHETHELELE
NKOSI
MDALI WEZULU[7]

Come Heal.
Trapeta B. Mayson

O Lord, all my longing is known to you;
    my sighing is not hidden from you.
My heart throbs, my strength fails me;
    as for the light of my eyes—it also has gone from me.
My friends and companions stand aloof from my affliction,
    and my neighbors stand far off.

Ps. 38:9–11

Contend, O LORD, with those who contend with me;
    fight against those who fight against me!
Take hold of shield and buckler,
    and rise up to help me!
Draw the spear and javelin
    against my pursuers;
say to my soul,
    "I am your salvation."

Ps. 35:1–3

I LONG TO BE

I long to be static free
Confusion, chaos free
I want to be around wash and wear folks
Just leave me on the line to dry on breezy days folks
I hate when people press me
Depress me, Oppress me, want to Suppress me
. . . .

I don't like drama, performances
Requiring costumes, clown attire, masks
Just leave me on the line to dry
On breezy days with other wash and wear folks

> I long to be
> Static free, confusion, chaos free
> No need to press me
> No need to press me
>
> Trapeta B. Mayson

Even though I walk through the darkest valley,
    I fear no evil;
for you are with me;
    your rod and your staff—they comfort me.

Ps. 23:4

Hear a just cause, O LORD; attend to my cry;
    give ear to my prayer from lips free of deceit.
From you let my vindication come;
    let your eyes see the right.

Guard me as the apple of [your] eye;
    hide me in the shadow of your wings,
from the wicked who despoil me,
    my deadly enemies who surround me.
They close their hearts to pity;
    with their mouths they speak arrogantly.

Ps. 17:1–2, 8–10

You [O God] have kept count of my tossings;
    put my tears in your bottle.

Ps. 56:8

How long, O LORD? Will you forget me forever?
    How long will you hide your face from me?
How long must I bear pain in my soul,
    and have sorrow in my heart all day long?
How long shall my enemy be exalted over me?

Ps. 13:1–2

On the day I called, you answered me,
    you increased my strength of soul.

Ps. 138:3

Let me abide in your tent forever,
    find refuge under the shelter of your wings.
Ps. 61:4

Over my head I hear music in the air
Over my head I hear music in the air
Over my head I hear music in the air,
There must be a God somewhere.
Traditional Spiritual

Hear my cry, O God;
    listen to my prayer.
From the end of the earth I call to you,
    when my heart is faint.
Lead me to the rock that is higher than I.
Ps. 61:1–2

Deliver me, O LORD, from evildoers;
protect me from those who are violent.
. . . .
Guard me, O LORD, from the hands of the wicked.
Ps. 140:1, 4

Be merciful to me, O God, be merciful to me,
    for in you my soul takes refuge;
in the shadow of your wings I will take refuge,
    until the destroying storms pass by.
Ps. 57:1

On my heart imprint your image,
Blessed Jesus, king of grace
That life's troubles nor its pleasures
Ever may your work erase;
Let the clear inscription be:
Jesus crucified for me,
Is my life, my hope's foundation,
All my glory and salvation!
Thomas H. Kingo
Translated by Peer O. Strömme[8]

O LORD, you have searched me and known me.
You know when I sit down and when I rise up;
   you discern my thoughts from far away.
You search out my path and my lying down,
   and are acquainted with all my ways.
. . . .
For it was you who formed my inward parts;
   you knit me together in my mother's womb.
I praise you, for I am fearfully and wonderfully made.
   Wonderful are your works;
that I know very well.

Ps. 139:1–3, 13–14

FOR SOME SISTERS

In spite of it all, we learned to love ourselves
We learned to face the wounds of the past
We now meet the wounds of the present, sometimes, they are stinging wounds,
Filled with salt
We learned to lick them real clean
We learned to let them heal
We are the women now
There is so much beauty in a sister who loves herself
We smile at ourselves when we can stand up straight without tipping over
We are balanced now
We look at this skin we're in
We can open our eyes wide and look at this here body
With the heavy thighs and the expanded hips and we do not tip over
We have reached equilibrium—We are women now.
. . . .
In spite of all the nonsense, we learned to love ourselves
In spite of folks telling us we ain't nothing, we think we all that,
We always got too much to say,
In spite of folks telling us we ain't light enough, ain't dark enough,
too black, too proud
In spite of all this, we learned to love ourselves
In spite of being dissed, pimped, displayed, violated, screwed without consent
We learned to love ourselves.
. . . .
There is so much beauty in a sister who loves herself
We are the women now
This poem is for all us sisters who smile
At ourselves every time we can stand up straight without tipping over
There is so much beauty in a sister who loves herself.

Trapeta B. Mayson

FOR FURTHER READING

J. Frank Henderson. *Liturgies of Lament.* Archdiocese of Chicago: Liturgy Training Publications, 1994.

National Organization for Victim Assistance, www.trynova.org.

Ann Weems. *Psalms of Lament.* Louisville, KY: Westminster John Knox Press, 1995.

Renita J. Weems. *Listening for God: A Minister's Journey through Silence and Doubt.* New York: Touchstone (Simon & Schuster, Inc.), 1999.

For Further Reading on Sexual Abuse and Healing

Kathleen D. Billman and Daniel L. Migliore. *Rachel's Cry: Prayer of Lament and Rebirth of Hope.* Cleveland: United Church Press, 1999.

Pamela Cooper-White. *The Cry of Tamar: Violence against Women and the Church's Response.* Minneapolis: Augsburg Fortress, 1995.

Mike Lew. *Victims No Longer: Men Recovering from Incest and Other Sexual Child Abuse.* New York: HarperCollins Publishers, 1988, 1990.

Renita J. Weems. *Battered Love: Marriage, Sex and Violence in the Hebrew Prophets.* Minneapolis: Fortress Press, 1995.

Mari West Zimmerman. *Take and Make Holy: Honoring the Sacred in the Healing Journey of Abuse Survivors.* Chicago: Liturgy Training Publications, 1995.

For Further Reading on Suicide

Diane Ackerman. *A Slender Thread: Rediscovering Hope at the Heart of Crisis.* New York: Vintage Books, 1997.

Corrine Chilstrom. *Andrew, You Died Too Soon: A Family Experience of Grieving and Living Again.* Minneapolis: Augsburg Fortress, 1993.

Carla Fine. *No Time to Say Goodbye: Surviving the Suicide of a Loved One.* New York: Doubleday, 1997.

Christine Smith. "Embracing the Windstorm." Pages 94–101 in *Sermons on Suicide.* Edited by James T. Clemons. Louisville, KY: Westminster Press, 1989.

Ann Smolin and John Guinan. *Healing after the Suicide of a Loved One.* New York: Fireside, 1993.

Chapter 5

Rituals for Recovery

We were lost in night,
But you sought and found us.
Give us strength to fight;
Death is all around us.
Jesus be our light.
                    *Muus Jacobse**

*F*aye found our church's number in the *Yellow Pages*. As a child she had been baptized in a sister church in our denomination, and she thought we were the church closest to her home, though she wasn't really sure. No matter: that day, our meeting seemed meant to be. We talked briefly. Faye told me she was alcoholic and wanted desperately to stop drinking. Would I pray with her?

She wanted to kneel. I prayed. I asked if she would like to take a new name to mark her turning into recovery. She chose "Mary," after the mother of Jesus, who had once said to an angel, "Here am I . . . let it be with me according to your word" (Luke 1:38). That simply, that mysteriously, Faye Mary moved into recovery—and she has not turned back. She believes that God led her to our church and into recovery and that God accompanies her through all the peaks and valleys of her journey in recovery. She is grateful. For her, "Mary" is a sign of all these things.

It is an awesome experience for a pastor to stand beside someone at the turning point, a rare one even in a congregation with many recovering people. The moment often follows years of struggle and failed attempts. At the moment of prayer with Faye, I didn't know if it would really be her turn into recovery. As

*"We Who Once Were Dead," © 1967, Gooi en Sticht, BV., Baarn, The Netherlands. All rights reserved. Exclusive agent for English-language countries: OCP Publications, 5536 NE Hassalo, Portland, OR 97213. Used with permission.

Faye's recovery grew and took hold, though, we both knew that we had witnessed God's almighty power working in her, through the ministry of our church.

Many churches allow 12-step programs to use their buildings. Yet in many of the worshiping congregations of those churches recovering people are nearly invisible. It is not simply addicts' self-consciousness, embarrassment, or shame that keeps many of them away from Christian churches, even when they are in recovery. While "All are welcome!" may grace the congregation's sign or stationery, those words often do not ring true for people struggling with addiction. They haven't felt themselves welcome in many Christian churches, which often unknowingly exude self-righteousness. It takes spiritual maturity for a congregation to welcome people struggling with addiction—to receive their presence and their gifts.

The rituals in this recovery cycle grow out of spiritual reflection on current medical and psychological practice that understands addiction as an illness needing treatment rather than as a moral failing. The rituals in this chapter provide resources for recovery across a wide spectrum—from active addiction through supporting life decades into recovery—and are appropriate whatever a person's "drug of choice." They are suggested here as part of *congregation's* ministry. How might such a ministry develop?

Pastors and church leaders do not always see them, but people struggling with addiction and in various stages of recovery are everywhere—church members who haven't shared that side of themselves, friends and family of church members, and neighbors. When churches provide public notice in their bulletins and newsletters that recovery resources are available, people who want assistance will identify themselves.

Two of the rituals in this cycle (Acknowledging Addiction and Affirmations for Recovery) work well for an addict's personal use, perhaps with a loved one or sponsor but without a pastor or worship leader. Prepare a brochure of recovery resources that includes these rituals, with a list of other kinds of recovery support available in your church or community. Include other rituals in this cycle that people might work on with a minister, the dates and times of 12-step programs, and the name of a pastor or other contact person. Display the brochure in a church fellowship area and in the rooms where recovery programs meet. People open to greater visibility and support will initiate contact.

CHRISTIAN MINISTRY AND 12-STEP PROGRAMS

There are other ways of addressing addiction and recovery, but many recovering people use 12-step programs. For that reason, and because there are natural connections between step work and Christian theology and practice, I want to note some of the links between the rituals presented here and the steps.[1]

First, Christian theology and 12-step recovery programs share the central belief that we do not save ourselves. At the program's essential core is step 1, the statement "We admitted that we were powerless over alcohol—that our lives had become unmanageable." "By grace you have been saved," says Ephesians 2:5. This is one of the places where 12-step programs' debt to Christian thought is clearest, says Tom Driver.[2]

Second, confession and forgiveness are the lifeblood of Christian practice, a practice that is also quite fitting in many aspects of recovery work. Consider steps 5–10, through which recovering addicts come to terms with how their actions have hurt others and then seek to make amends for them. In essence, an addict makes a confession, seeks forgiveness, then sets out to live in newness of life.

When we understand addiction as an illness requiring treatment, though, there's one place where we will want to be careful not to insist on confession and forgiveness: at the time of a relapse. Recovery is precarious, punctuated by relapses and marked by moments of wonder and surprise. Relapses are the rule, not the exception, especially in the months and years leading up to the real turn into recovery. Understanding this context helps ease the shame associated with sliding off recovery's path.

Third, with resurrection and new life among Christianity's core beliefs, Christian belief and practice provide a framework for understanding relapse and the possibility of new beginnings. Rooted in the love of a gracious God, Christian teaching provides an antidote to an addict's feelings of unworthiness and self-loathing as well as encouragement simply to return to the work of recovery.

Fourth, including a ministry of recovery in a church's ministry counters people's natural tendency to isolate themselves when their behavior spins out of control. The public availability of the rituals announces, "People with addiction problems are welcome in church. You may come here when you are struggling, *even with these things*. And you are not the only one."

Fifth, a visible recovery ministry serves as a witness to those who are struggling with abuse and addiction but are not yet able to take the first steps themselves into recovery. It signals their welcome in the congregation and the congregation's openness to stand with them when they are ready to take greater responsibility for their addictive behavior. Marking anniversaries of sobriety shows the congregation's investment in the addict's recovery: "It is important also *for us* that you are recovering from addiction."

Finally, including recovery rituals in a congregation's ministry makes that ministry more whole: ministry is about healing, connection, and standing with people where they are. Given how many struggle with addiction, support for recovery is a necessity in a church's ministry.

The worship resources in this cycle don't take the place of treatment for addiction; they can't. What ritual can do, however, is both to enact the movement into recovery and to embody recovery. To enact the movement into recovery is to act out, as though on a stage, externally, a movement that is happening inside the participant. Taking a new name, she symbolizes the turn into recovery that is already stirring within her. To embody recovery in a ritual is to act out now the life the recovering person is working toward. Thus by acting honestly and responsibly in a ritual to let go of the habit of socializing in bars, for instance, the process of planning and doing the ritual with integrity already models the participant's continued growth in recovery and the new life that he hopes the ritual will further help him to achieve.

These rituals seek to make the gifts of recovery visible—the gift of choices that nurture life, the gift of gratitude, the gift of the present moment, even when it is painful, the gift of strength and responsibility. Offer these rituals for your community's use and your ministry will also be blessed in many ways. You will help some people who struggle with addiction to find and keep a new life, and their lives will enrich your congregation with many gifts.

ACKNOWLEDGING ADDICTION

Give me a candle of the Spirit, O God, as I go down into the deeps of my being. Show me the hidden things, the creatures of my dreams, the storehouse of forgotten memories and hurts. Take me down to the spring of my life and tell me my nature and my name. Give me freedom to grow, so that I may become that self, the seed of which you planted in me at my making. Out of the deeps I cry to you, O God.
George Appleton[3]

Addiction is filled with denial ("I could stop if I wanted to stop"); with despair; with self-loathing and a sense of unworthiness; with feelings of powerlessness and hopelessness; and with increasing isolation from family, friends, and other support. At the same time, even in addiction's deepest throes, addicts report glimmers of self-understanding and a longing for healing—glimmers, unfortunately, that soon get extinguished again in denial.

This ritual plants a seed. It is one step along the way: a getting ready to be ready to stop.

An addict may begin to voice concern about his drug use or sexual acting out years before he can turn into recovery and stay on that path. The intervening time can be especially challenging for loved ones nearby. They watch addiction's grip tightening its hold, but when they try to speak of it with the person, they are often met with fierce denial. Many who stand nearby, including ministers and other church leaders, long to be able to "do something" to help as someone's addiction spins out of control. Yet just those well-meaning urges often undermine the addict's own action, which is primary to the healing of recovery. This first ritual offers an appropriate role for those closest to an addict.

In some cases a pastor may be close to someone struggling with addiction, but more often it will be a family member, church member, or friend—someone who is already important in the addict's life—who will be able to share this ritual with him or her. Notes in chapter 5's introduction provide suggestions for how pastors and other worship leaders might make these materials available in their congregation and community.

The person leading this ritual becomes a kind of prayer partner to the one struggling with addiction. As prayer partner, she stands beside the one who is struggling, bringing a word of faith and hope to what often feels desperate and impossible. This brief ritual offers a glimpse of the promise of recovery to the one who is struggling—of speaking a difficult truth instead of hiding it; of finding support instead of isolating from others in shame; of staying with difficult feelings rather than numbing them with addictive substances or behaviors.

The ritual's power comes simply from speaking and listening, an interchange that is more powerful than one might assume. Once something is spoken aloud between two people, it is harder to make the words disappear, harder to swallow them up later as though they had never been spoken. The interchange of speaking and listening helps to break the addict's cycle of isolation and hiding. Listening to the addict's own cries and reflecting them back to him affirms his own self-awareness of his problems. Once the problem has been named, the one serving as a prayer partner bears witness to the presence of God by offering a Bible verse, and the seed of the hope of recovery is planted.

SAYING IT OUT LOUD:
GETTING READY TO BE READY TO STOP

Unlike most rituals, it won't be possible to plan out this ritual's time and place in advance. The ritual is initiated when the addict speaks with some self-awareness of his or her problems.

The person serving as prayer partner already knows the person struggling with addiction and has witnessed that person crying out for help. To prepare for a moment that will arise in its own time, the one leading this ritual reflects in advance on scriptural passages that could speak of God's presence with the one who is struggling.

It is important to note that the ritual does not exact promises from the addict that she is not ready yet to make. Nor does the one with the addict make wishful promises he won't later be able to keep. Primarily, the listening one bears witness to what the addict says and is feeling and speaks that aloud.

Choose a Scripture verse to give to the one struggling with addiction. Consider passages that speak of God's presence, strength, or power to call forth new life. Write out the verse and carry it with you.

SUGESTIONS FOR SCRIPTURE READINGS: Deut. 33:27 (KJV); Ps. 119:105; Isa. 43:1–3; Matt. 6:34; 11:28; 18:20; Luke 1:78–79; John 1:5.

LISTENING AND REFLECTING BACK
When a moment arrives that the addict names worries about life spinning out of control, take note of where you are and whether there are others around who might overhear. If you are not in a private place, suggest that you move:

> **Leader:** Could we step into that room over there? I'd like to respond to you in a more private setting.

Listen to what the person says as she or he cries out. When she or he has finished speaking, say:

> **Leader:** I would like to surround your words with silence for a moment.

[*pause*]

> **Leader:** Would you say it again, what you have said?

After she or he speaks, and after another pause, reflect back to her or him, saying:

Leader: I want you to know that I have heard you. You said that
[*paraphrase his/her words*].

SHARING A WORD
*Give the person the Bible verse you have written out in advance on the card,
reading it aloud as you hand it to him or her, or read it aloud together.*

Leader: I have chosen this word for you as a sign of God's presence
with you in this difficulty, and of God's calling you forth
into new life.

*If you feel ready to do so, you may offer your support as the person attempts
to move into recovery. If you are unsure about your ability to take this on, skip
this step.*

Leader: I would like to stand with you when you are ready to seek
help for [*the problem that he or she has named, using his or
her own words*].

If offering prayer feels appropriate and the person agrees, close with prayer.

Leader: May we pray together as we leave this place?

Out of the depths we cry to you, O Lord. Lord, hear our cry.
We thank you for the truth that [*Name*] has put into words just
now, for *his/her* courage in speaking it out loud. Be a source
of strength as *he/she* prepares now to act on this truth. By
your mighty power, bring your healing to [*Name*] and carry
him/her into recovery. We ask in Jesus' name. **Amen.**

᠄᠄᠄᠄᠄᠄᠄

TURNING INTO RECOVERY

*So God created humankind in his image,
in the image of God he created them;
male and female he created them.*
                              Gen. 1:27

In some Christian traditions, young people who are about to be confirmed
may take on a new name as a sign of their faith and of greater responsibility

in the life of their Christian community. In my work with people struggling with addiction and in various stages of recovery, I have discovered that taking on a new name can also be an important spiritual tool to support addicts' work in recovery.

The move into recovery from addiction is especially well-suited for such a ritual. The ritual act of taking on a new name can be a way to be called forth into a new life of recovery or a way to remember that new life. The old life of addiction and the new life in recovery are opposing forces. The temptation to be drawn back to the old life is often fierce. An addict who takes a new name stakes a claim with the new life of recovery.

The work of recovery from addiction is partly about rediscovering and honoring a truer self, a self created in the image of God, though it is barely recognizable in the downward spiral of addiction. In this context, a new name is a witness to God's transcendent power to break the hold of addiction on a person's life, a sign of the person's worth before God and a sign of the addict's desire to live in recovery.

A new name is capable of symbolizing what many addicts experience as a divine reversal in their lives, which many describe as mysterious, grace-filled, and unexpected. Ian Frazier tells a story of that kind of reversal in *On the Rez: Modern Tales of Ordinary Life and Extraordinary Valor in the Hard Land of the Oglala Sioux*. SuAnne Big Crow had traveled with her high school basketball team to Lead, South Dakota, where Indians like them, from the reservation, worried about their safety. From the locker room, they heard Lead fans mixing their cheers with derisive taunts—yelling fake Indian war cries, taunting their opponents about welfare. Leading her team out onto the court

> SuAnne went right down the middle and suddenly stopped when she got to center court. . . . [and] began to do the Lakota shawl dance. . . . And then she started to sing . . . in Lakota, swaying back and forth in the jump-ball circle, doing the shawl dance, using her warm-up jacket for a shawl. The crowd went completely silent.
>
> "All that stuff the Lead fans were yelling—it was like she *reversed* it somehow," a teammate says. In the sudden quiet all they could hear was her Lakota song. . . . [Then] the audience began to cheer.[4]

It was, says Frazier, "elegant, generous, transcendent . . . inviting the jeering crowd [to know the true Lakota]."[5]

Pastors know how to pray, and they know when prayer is appropriate. Prayer is one of the spiritual tools of their ministry. Offering the opportunity for someone to choose a new name can also be a spiritual tool of ministry, and a sign of the reversal of recovery life. Consider biblical stories about people with a particular strength or character that remind you of the person with you. Choose several possibilities, briefly telling the biblical story. Then open the conversation for the person to make other suggestions. From a few choices I offered Joyce, who had struggled with addiction for decades, she chose Elizabeth, a name that reminded her that God could carry her through many years of barrenness and then bring her to new life (Luke 1). Faye chose Mary, remembering how Jesus' mother spoke with an angel. Family names or the names of saints might also work well symbolically.

Taking a new name—and recalling it, bearing it, living with it—support the ongoing daily work of recovery. Once someone has taken on a new name, for instance, a person may want to find ways of using it, whether or not he or she decides to change the name legally. Use of a recovery name is suggested in other rituals found in this cycle. Mention of the new name on recovery anniversaries, for example, reaffirms the new life in recovery, no matter how far along in recovery one is. Its use after a slip also reaffirms life in recovery as well as God's constancy through peaks and valleys.

᠅᠅᠅᠅᠅᠅᠅

A NEW NAME

In the course of ongoing pastoral conversation between someone strug-gling with addiction and his or her pastor, a pastor may notice an occasion when taking on a new name in a ritual could be a helpful sign of the turn into recovery. Some people may initiate the possibility of a name change them-selves. The ritual offered here arose in conversation like that, and it took place right then, without further planning.

Even if the ritual arises extemporaneously in pastoral conversation, the person being given a new name has a crucial role. She or he should decide, for example, whether to proceed with choosing and taking a name right then; whether to plan to do it on another occasion; how to choose a name; and, often, what the name will be. The person's active participation allows the meaning and significance of the name to grow. Some will want another per-son—a pastor, relative, or friend—to choose a name for them or with them. Others will find the act of choosing and announcing the choice the very rea-son for doing such a ritual: "This is me as I know myself."

The ritual may also be used after a person is already in recovery, as a sign of an earlier turning into recovery. In that case, allow the person to choose a time and place that bear some significance to the turn into recovery. Let him or her decide whether others might be invited to be present. If the person's name will be changed legally, the ritual might be used before or after the court proceedings.

Although this use would be the exception rather than the rule, especially among those still struggling with addiction, the naming ritual may be inserted as part of the regular worship of a congregation. If so, place it at the time of congregational prayers. See the alternate version available for that purpose below.

When the event is planned in advance, gifts, perhaps ones with the new name on them, may also be appropriate. If the new name is biblical, a new Bible might be appropriate, with the story of the biblical person marked. Other gifts might highlight the person's strengths or the circumstances of the turning.

Beyond recovery from addiction, this ritual also works well at certain other significant moments in a person's life: in coming out of jail, for instance, or in joining the church after a long time away.

However small the gathering, some form of shared meal afterward is almost always appropriate. Sharing food builds community. It provides an occasion to sit and dwell for a moment in the hopes of the day.

A second alternate version of this ritual is offered for devotional use. The person taking on the new name may commit these words to memory and use them as prayer-like personal affirmation using the new name. As such, it may be part of regular daily devotions, or may be used when the person is having a particularly rough day. See the final exercise in chapter 7 (pp. 183–87) for guidance on helping someone prepare affirmations as a spiritual discipline.

OPENING

The leader briefly acknowledges the occasion for which the person takes a new name: for example, "As she joins the church this morning, Joyce takes on a new middle name as a sign of the new life God has opened up to her in recovery from addiction"; or "Ben has just finished serving his time in jail. He takes on a new name as a sign [among all of us] that he intends never again to go behind those walls"; or, set in the context of prayer, "O God, you hear Faye's cries for help as she struggles with her addiction to alcohol. We come before Your throne of grace this day asking that by Your mighty arm You might help her turn into recovery. We ask that her taking a new name for recovery be a sign before You of her desire to be made well. Amen."

Leader: The apostle Paul never saw Jesus in his earthly ministry, nor was he from Jerusalem, two sure signs, some believed, that he could not be an apostle of Jesus Christ. Paul retorts, "I am the least of the apostles, unfit to be called an apostle, because I persecuted the church of God. But by the grace of God I am what I am, and [God's] grace toward me has not been in vain" (1 Cor. 15:9–10).

Let us pray: We praise You, O God, for the gift of life and of new life. Especially this day, we praise you for the gifts of [*Name*], created by your power and grace. Nurture this turn into recovery in *her/him*. (*If the person is returning from jail or joining the church after a long time away, name those circumstances.*) Strengthen *her/his* faith. Lead *her/him* in *her/his* walk of new life. We ask in Jesus' name.

All: Amen.

The leader reads aloud one or more lessons from Scripture. The person being named may want to choose and/or read one.

SUGGESTIONS FOR SCRIPTURE READINGS: Gen. 1:27; 17:1–8; 17:15–16 [17–21]; 32:22–30; Isa. 43:1–7; Jer. 1:4–8; Luke 1:57–66; 2:8–21; Rom. 12:1–2; Eph. 6:10–20; 1 John 3:1–2.

THE NAMING CEREMONY

Leader: This *man/woman* shall now be called [*new name*].

[*Or*]

**The Person
Being Named:** I would like you to call me [*new name*].

All: *We/I* call you [*Name*].

The person being named, or another, explains the meaning of the chosen name. The others present affirm the new name. Unless the new name replaces a given name, use both names.

Leader: [*Old and new names*], we call you by name. May you know yourself beloved and cherished by God, and esteemed in our company.

All: Amen.

Those present may mark the occasion by giving a gift.

> **Leader:** Receive this gift as a sign of this day and of all your hopes for this new beginning.

> **All: Amen.**

PRAYER AND BENEDICTION
Prayers may be offered appropriate to the situation. The Lord's Prayer may conclude the prayers.

> **Leader:** Gracious God, fountain of new life, we bless you for the gift of [*Name's*] turning [*this day*]. We thank you for your arms of love, for making a way out of no way, and for the name [*Name name*], sign of new life in You. Bless [*Name*], we ask you, in Jesus' name. **Amen.**

The service (or this part of the service, if it is placed in the context of a larger service) concludes with the Peace. A hymn or song may be sung.

> **Leader:** The peace of the Lord be with you always.

> **All: And also with you.**

HYMN SUGGESTIONS

"Changed Mah Name"
"I Will Do a New Thing in You"
"O God, Our Help in Ages Past"
"How Firm a Foundation"
"The Lord Is My Light"
"I Want Jesus to Walk with Me"
"Oh, Let the Son of God Enfold You"
"We've Come This Far by Faith"
"You Satisfy the Hungry Heart"

A NEW NAME: ALTERNATE VERSION FOR USE IN PUBLIC WORSHIP

A recovering person might want some public acknowledgment of taking a new name. If so, this prayer petition can be offered in the congregation's worship, at prayer time. It may serve either as a public acknowledgment of the more private ritual, or as the ritual itself in a simplified form. If the prayer serves as the ritual itself, spend time in pastoral conversation beforehand choosing a name and considering how to make public notice about the event in the bulletin or announcements.

People in recovery often struggle mightily against pride as a force that can undermine their recovery. This prayer appeals to God, whose strength makes recovery possible. Avoid actions around the prayer, like calling the person forward or concluding the prayer with applause, that draw undue attention to the person.

Leader: O God, Author and Giver of all life: it was You who formed our inward parts, You who knit us together in our mothers' wombs (Ps. 139:13). You call us each by name. As [*original name*] comes this day to take a new name, [*new name*], as a sign of [*reason for new name, e.g., recovery from addiction*], we ask that you strengthen and encourage *her/him*. Be the light on *her/his* path, the hand that leads *her/him*. We ask in Jesus' name.

All: Amen.

❦❦❦❦❦❦❦

DEVOTIONAL USE OF A NEW NAME

This personal affirmation may be repeated as part of a daily or occasional remembrance by the person who has taken a new name.

By the grace of God, I am who I am. I am *called/named* [*new name*]. Keep me, O God, this day, on the path of recovery [*or on the path that will keep me out of prison, or other appropriate phrase*].

❦❦❦❦❦❦❦

AFFIRMATIONS TO NURTURE
THE NEW LIFE OF RECOVERY

Keep these words. . . . talk about them when you are at home
and when you are away, when you lie down and when you rise.
                                                      Deut. 6:6, 7

To establish a rhythm for daily life, to be carried through life's most difficult passageways, to quell deeply rooted negative voices inside, to remember that in each moment we stand in the presence of God: these are the function and purposes of affirmations used as a discipline of Christian faith. Affirmations also offer important daily support for someone who is in recovery from addiction.

Consider first how affirmations work in the life of faith apart from recovery work. This affirmation from Frederic Shaffmaster combines words from Scripture with traditional and free prayer:

> Divine will is all-powerful.
> Divine will is truth, is good, is love. . . .
> Our Heavenly Father strengthen my faith,
>   the faith that makes me whole.
> Help me to love and return love. . . .
> Help me to be still and know that Thou art God [Ps. 46:10].
> I believe, help Thou my unbelief [Mark 9:24].
> Thy will, not mine, be done [Jesus' words from Gethsemane,
> Mark 14:36, also picked up in the Lord's Prayer, Matt. 6:10].
>   Frederic Shaffmaster[6]

When Frederic repeats these words, now long committed to memory, the kernels of faith strung together mark the rhythm of his life, day in and day out. They help him find his own life's meaning living inside their words. In times of difficulty, they reorient him by turning him back to God. Affirmations are often like creeds, that is, brief statements of faith that, when spoken, feel like a prayer.

Recovery begins when someone stops drinking, stops taking drugs, or turns away from self-destructive behavior like gambling, overeating, or acting promiscuously. But the new life of recovery takes years to develop roots and mature. It is a lifelong task. In the rooms of many 12-step programs, affirmations are the lifeblood of the new life of recovery and part of being created anew. One addict told me that during the whole first year of recovery, only one affirmation arose—I am a human being—and she could barely speak that affirmation. But it was a beginning.

When affirmations arise from inside, as they did for this person, instead of being prescribed by a set program or order, the new life of recovery is being created from a place where it can take hold and grow. Affirmations, like the work of the twelve steps themselves, seem to find the addict as he or she is open to them. Recovery is a process of learning to listen to the voice inside, which is the place from which affirmations arise. Out of their experience guiding parishioners in prayer and in faith formation, ministers can encourage their people who struggle with addiction and recovery to listen to that voice inside and to develop their own affirmations. Creating affirmations is a spiritual exercise some use to build strength in recovery. For discussions of how to help someone develop affirmations, see the discussion in chapter 7 (pp. 183–87).

THE OTHER SIDE—INCLUDING LAMENTATIONS

Modern-day affirmations tend to be positive statements of fact. One line of Roy Oswald's "Personal Affirmation," for instance, says, "Everywhere I go I am loved and supported by others."[7] Biblical blessings, on the other hand, like the ones in Luke 6:20–26, express both the positive and the negative, blessing and lamentation. People in recovery often need to express both sides. The discussion in chapter 7 provides additional examples of affirmations and lamentations for recovery.

Be aware that self-reflection focusing on lamentations often opens up a deep and abiding sorrow. So many losses are associated with the years of active addiction—years of life lost; lost opportunities to love others appropriately; regret and grief about the impact of addiction on others and for the recovering addict.

෬෬෬෬෬෬෬

RECOVERY AFFIRMATIONS I: LAMENTATIONS AND BLESSINGS

Affirmations are designed for a recovering person to use alone at a regular time each day. They may also be repeated at other times as necessary, during particularly hard moments—as, for example, when feeling the urge to drink. They may also help as physical reminders pasted on a mirror or the refrigerator, or above the computer. To use these affirmations:

- *Choose a regular part of your day or your week when you can focus on building your life in recovery. When affirmations become a regular part of your life, they will come to mind when you need them in a time of crisis.*
- *Choose a regular place inside or outside to say your affirmations, a place where you will be able to relax and where you will not be disturbed.*
- *Do not hurry. Use the pauses to slow down the pace.*
- *Use the affirmations by themselves, or the lamentations and affirmations together. You may also include them as part of a broader devotional time in a form like the one printed out below.*

If lamentations are used with affirmations, as they are here, they precede the blessings. Then the experience of the negative and positive together follows the pattern of confession and forgiveness, and the emphasis falls on the power of God to bring forth new life.

Biblical blessings are written "Blessed are you . . ." or "Blessed is the one. . . ." In affirmations, the speaker takes these on personally: "Blessed am I . . ." or "Woe to me. . . ."

SETTLING IN
Begin with a moment of silence to center yourself in the present moment, then read or recite a Bible verse.

SUGGESTIONS FOR SCRIPTURE READINGS: Gen. 2:7; Ps. 27:1; 31:3–5; 46:10; Isa. 58:11; Lam. 3:21–23; Josh. 24:15; Matt. 6:25, 6:34 (RSV); John 20:21; 1 Cor. 15:10

LAMENTATIONS
Slowly read or recite the lamentations first, if you use them:

Woe to me when I lie to cover myself.
Woe to me when I isolate myself and burn my bridges with others.
Woe to me when I pretend that my addiction is not a problem.
Woe to me when I act as though I am powerless to change the circumstances of my life.

[*pause*]

But I want to live in recovery this day.

(*Or:*) But God has blessed me with a life in recovery and I want to cherish this day.

[*pause*]

AFFIRMATIONS
Slowly read or recite the affirmations.

> Blessed am I when I can acknowledge that I stand in the presence of God, who can restore me to sanity.
> Blessed am I when I turn my life over to God today.
> Blessed am I when I can be honest with myself about who I am, even about my shortcomings.
> Blessed am I when I can make amends today for anyone that I have harmed.
> Blessed am I when I can turn my heart to the work of recovery in these ways: [*Name the ways that are important to you.*]

Spend a moment in silence.

Close with a song, if desired.

HYMN SUGGESTIONS

> "Breathe on Me, Breath of God"
> "O God, Our Help in Ages Past"
> "Lead Me, Guide Me"
> "This Is the Day"
> "Great Is Thy Faithfulness"
> "All Night, All Day, Angels Watching over Me"

RECOVERY AFFIRMATIONS II:
BREATHING THE NEW LIFE OF RECOVERY

These affirmations were developed from the stories and life experiences of many whom I have known moving from addiction to recovery. They are rooted in "I," in the present moment, and incorporate deep breathing for relaxation.
Follow the suggestions for time and place given with the first recovery affirmations. These affirmations may stand alone. If you want to place them into

a broader personal devotional time, insert them in place of the Lamentations and Affirmations sections of the first ritual.

These recovery affirmations depend as much on the power of breath as on the power of words. Breathing deeply allows participants to relax, to let go of bothersome thoughts, and to receive the gift of peace. If you find it hard to enter into relaxation, consider inviting someone like your pastor or a prayer partner to lead you through the opening breathing exercise until you learn how to breathe more deeply on your own.

SETTLING IN
Begin by sitting in a comfortable spot. Close your eyes. Feel the support of your chair beneath you. Inhale deeply and exhale fully, and breathe evenly until you feel your breath slowing down and your body relaxing into your chair.

BREATH AND AFFIRMATION
Speak the following words aloud slowly from memory, or read them if you haven't yet memorized them.

I have known the curse of addiction.
[*Or:*] I am [*an alcoholic/a drug addict*].
[*Or:*] [*Food/gambling/sexual acting out*] has been my drug of choice.
I have numbed myself on [*alcohol/drugs/food/shopping/sex*] so that I
    could feel nothing.
I have lied and stolen.
I have held myself apart even from the ones who love me, until I was all
    alone.

[*Pause. Breathe.*]

But this day I am in recovery.

[*Pause. Breathe.*]

I feel grateful for this day of recovery.
I have been given this day, full of hope and promise, and I may choose
    how to live it.
I feel pain and anxiety, but now I also know joy and laughter.
I am strong.
I am capable.
I am connected with others.

I can ask for help when I need it.
I am a child of God, and God loves me.

[*Pause. Breathe.*]

I am grateful for this day of recovery.

[*Pause. Breathe.*]

LIVING INTO YOUR DELIVERANCE

*It's not the words of the service that I recall, but what I did with my
body, where I moved, how I knelt, how I stretched out my hands. . . .
My mind . . . was able to grasp very little of what the service was all
about. For the time being, my intellect needed to step aside and
observe in silence, so that my body could lead the way.*
                                        Margaret Bullitt-Jonas[8]

As significant as the turn into recovery is—the moment, the day—it marks
only recovery's birth. Recovery unfolds, deepens, and grows. In the context
of turning one's life over to God, recovery is a twofold task: taking on the life
of recovery and letting go of the old life of addiction. It is saying yes to life
and no to all that works against life. Yet patterns of addiction are at times so
deeply ingrained that letting go is not a simple or natural process. The letting-
go ritual is a physical enactment of turning away from a particular aspect of
a person's old life in addiction. It is less about the words spoken and more
about a body enacting letting go.

Hear a piece of fabric tearing. That sound got me thinking about how to rit-
ualize letting go of old patterns of addiction. Ripping out deeply rooted dys-
functional patterns may be healing, but first it is disturbing. Whatever the final
healing, ripping hurts.

Part of the work of recovery is learning how to feel pain, anguish, anger,
loss, and other difficult emotions without covering them up or medicating
them away. A second aspect of recovery's work involves learning how to set
appropriate boundaries. Addicts learn how to do these things and to grow into
their deliverance from others who are farther along in recovery, from therapy, through participation in 12-step programs, and through the use of other

spiritual disciplines like prayer and meditation. Ritual and its preparation can also help in this work. Our best worship customs allow us to express difficult feelings within a context of faith and community that puts limits on them and sets them in a wider context. Ritual can help us discover a container for newly felt, difficult emotions.

Consider, as an example, an Orthodox Jewish mourning custom. Writing about Jewish mourning customs, Ruben Schindler notes that Jewish law requires the bereaved to mourn his or her loss. Upon hearing the news of a loved one's death, and prior to interment, Orthodox custom provides encouragement for mourners to rend their garments. No mere ceremony, says Schindler, tearing garments "allows the mourner to give expression to his deep anger by means of a controlled, religiously sanctioned, act of destruction." Yet there are limits to the raw emotions: only the mourner him or herself may do the tearing, within a specific time frame. And cutting one's body or ripping hair is specifically prohibited.[9]

This ritual enacts letting go of a self-destructive behavior or habit of addiction. Though it requires more preparation than appears in this example, its movement and purpose are similar to an experience of Caroline Knapp's. When she had been sober for about six months, a friend visited Knapp in her home. Together they cut apart a black Lycra dress, a dress she hated but wore to please her boyfriend. It was a sign for her of a deeply alcoholic time, a time of self-loathing when she felt miserable and insecure. Destroying the dress became symbolic for her of letting go of measuring herself through other people's eyes. It was an essential moment in her growth in recovery.[10]

Destroying clothing is a symbolic action that illustrates the effort required to turn away from the most difficult aspects of addiction's old patterns. To stand with and for life means at some level to reject death and the forces of death that suffocate life.

The opportunity for the letting-go ritual arises, perhaps in pastoral conversation, when the recovering person is struggling with a particular vulnerability, when old patterns of addiction press hard upon him. It will probably be most helpful not at the first flush of turning into recovery but as recovery grows, and as it becomes apparent where the points of resistance lie. Recovering addicts prepare for the ritual by working with a minister or spiritual friend. Together they discuss the behavior or pattern of addiction that presses heavily upon the recovering person. Through conversation they choose an appropriate symbol and symbolic action for letting go. As in the Jewish mourning ritual, this symbol and symbolic action belong to the recovering person. Another may help him or her to discern an appropriate symbol, but the symbol will not work unless it resonates with his or her own struggles. For further discussion of the role of symbols in worship and for help in choosing appropriate symbols, see exercises in chapter 7 (173–77).

Also like the Jewish mourning ritual, the symbolic action of destruction in the letting-go ritual is set within the wider context of the recovering addict's life, faith, and bonds of love with others. The leader working with the recovering person and that person, as well as any other loved ones present, form a circle around the fire by locking hands on wrists. If holding on to others is uncomfortable for the recovering person, simply standing around the fire in a circle will also work. They mark a physical boundary around the fire together. At the end of the ritual, the fire is extinguished, limiting its destruction to a set time and place. All gathered share a meal and rejoice together after the rite. Thus the fire and the burning become a controlled, religiously sanctioned act of destruction. Raw emotions are present, yet they are held within limits and used to enhance the life of recovery.

LETTING GO OF AN ADDICTIVE BEHAVIOR

Pastors and others who know the person in recovery are best suited to lead this rite. Family members rarely have the combination of closeness and distance required.

It is crucial for this ritual that the recovering person be part of the planning. Then the planning process itself helps him or her learn how to give voice to his or her own needs. See the discussion in chapter 7 about choosing appropriate symbols and symbolic action (pp. 173–77).

Choose a place to hold the ritual that is appropriate to the symbolic action chosen. Burning clothing wouldn't work in a church building, for instance. The acts of removing something from a recovering person's closet or home by taking it to the dump, for another example, or of digging a hole to bury something, imply their own set settings.

If burning materials, choose a safe place, like a brick fire area in a park or a backyard barbecue grill.

This is not a ritual for a crowd. It could work with just the recovering person and a leader, or have the recovering person invite a few close friends, perhaps a 12-step sponsor or someone else further along in the process of recovery.

Conclude with a meal or refreshments to celebrate the movement more deeply into recovery.

The leader faces the recovering person, or, if more are present, gathers participants into a circle and begins with these words:

> **Leader:** We're here this afternoon to be witnesses with [*Name*] as *she/he* sets aside part of *her/his* old life of addiction. Hear these words of the apostle Paul:
>
>> Therefore, if anyone is in Christ, he is a new creation; the old has passed away, behold, the new has come. (2 Cor. 5:17 RSV)
>
> We are here to bear witness to the destruction of a part of [*Name's*] old life in addiction, that *his/her* new life in recovery might continue to flourish and grow.

The recovering person speaks of what he or she is leaving behind, and why this action about to be performed symbolizes what he or she is leaving behind.

> **Leader:** When you are ready to let go of this part of your past, light the fire. [*Or name other chosen symbolic action.*]

The recovering person lights the fire. When the fire is hot enough, she or he puts the article of clothing on the fire. While the fire burns, if it seems appropriate to the recovering person, the leader and she or he lock hands on wrists with each other and with others, if present, around the fire. The leader recites these verses, from memory, if possible:

> **Leader:** For everything there is a season . . .
> a time to break down, and a time to build up . . .
> a time to tear, and a time to sew. (Eccl. 3:1, 3, 7)

Keep silence to watch the fire burn. Then the leader may begin to sing something softly that people can sing without hymnbooks or papers in front of them. Or have one person call out a line and the others respond. Alternate silence and singing. Do not hurry.

HYMN SUGGESTIONS

"I Will Do a New Thing in You"
"Go Down, Moses" ("Let my people go!"), refrain only

"Taste and See," refrain only, or another hymn from Taizé
"Thy Word Is a Lamp," refrain only

CLOSING PRAYER AND SHARING PEACE
When the clothing has burned completely, the recovering person extinguishes the fire with water or a shovelful of dirt. The others gathered may help. The leader prays:

> **Leader:** O God of power and might, we bless you for the liberation of your children from every kind of bondage. Especially this day, we praise you for your work in [*Name's*] life, for releasing *him/her* from the bondage to addiction to [*Name his/her addiction*]. By your power to create new lives in Jesus, make of this day a turning point, we ask you, that [*Name*] may be set free from part of *his/her* addictive past, especially as *she/he* has known it in [*Name the behavior being left behind*]. We ask in Jesus' name.

> **All: Amen.**

Participants conclude with the sharing of the peace with each other.

> **Leader:** The peace of Christ be with you always.

> **All: And also with you.**

Participants share a meal together to celebrate the gift of new life that is growing in this one.

༽༽༽༽༽

BEGINNING AGAIN AFTER A SLIP

> *Great is Thy faithfulness!*
> *Great is Thy faithfulness!*
> *Morning by morning new mercies I see;*
> *All I have needed Thy hand hath provided,*
> *"Great is Thy faithfulness," Lord unto me!*
> *Thomas O. Chisholm*[11]

In a ritual of beginning again, the one who has slipped is given permission for and is helped to step back into recovery, to begin again. Addiction is a disease of recurrence; relapses are the norm, not the exception—especially in the years it takes to get to long-term maintenance in recovery.[12] Nevertheless, relapses take many recovering people by surprise and shake them at their foundation. Slips often engender disappointment, self-doubt, self-loathing, or despair for weeks or months afterward. Some slips lead back into more years of active addiction; some happen after years in recovery. After a slip, it is hard to believe in oneself and in the capacity to start again.

In one sense, starting over does require a whole new beginning—but it is a beginning that builds on time already spent in recovery. If the person had earlier chosen a new name at the start of recovery, using the name again here will remind him or her of the recovery work that has already been done. This three-part ritual allows the person to turn back into recovery through a period of meditation and reflection, by naming the slip aloud, and by an opportunity for recommitment. The recommitment section asks for God's blessing and support on this new beginning. When the leader speaks a gracious word from God at the recommitment, it is offered to counter the addict's intense feelings of unworthiness and self-doubt.

Repeated slips from recovery fill an addict with embarrassment or shame and the tendency to isolate. The person leading this ritual can acknowledge that truth while also making note of how common slips are. Mention before starting the ritual that should another slip occur—even if it's more than one slip—it would be possible to repeat the ritual briefly, selecting perhaps one section, reading, and song that are significant for that person.

⌖⌖⌖⌖⌖⌖⌖

RITUAL FOR USE AFTER A SLIP

This ritual is designed for use by someone who has been in recovery but has slipped back to patterns of the old life, even if only once. The ritual should be led by a pastor, a spiritual friend, or a mentor, but not by a family member or very close friend, for these emotional connections are too complicated. Ordinarily, this ritual would include just the leader and the person who has slipped.

This is not a ritual of confession and forgiveness. See the introduction of this chapter to explore this thought.

The ritual should be conducted in a safe place, at a time when there will be no interruptions. If it seems appropriate and the person has positive associations with a sanctuary or chapel, going to a place of worship might strengthen the tie with other experiences of new beginnings. Other settings might include a retreat setting or the person's home.

To prepare for the ritual, the leader should reflect with the participant about when and where to hold the ritual and about whether to sing together, whether to do an anointing with oil at the time of the benediction, and whether to take a new name for recovery, if the participant has not already done so. If the participant is not comfortable with anointing, the words at that point may simply be read aloud as a benediction. Preparations should also include reflection with the person about how she or he wants to answer the questions in the section "Naming the Slip Aloud."

The readings in the Meditation section are meant to be a time of reflection. Allow at least three to four minutes of silence after each reading; do not rush. The readings are set up to be read aloud alternately, between leader and participant, but the leader may also read them all. The participant may comment on one or more of the readings as they proceed or at the end of the readings. With silence between the readings and time for comment the ritual takes about an hour.

Some people find it helpful to have a memento of the turn back into recovery. The leader may print out the readings in a blank journal, one to a page, and include the remainder of the ritual, signing and dating it. Then the participant has some tangible reminder of the day of the step back into recovery. Alternatively, the leader may want to present a small gift at the end of the worship experience, a small cross, for instance, to remind the participant of the power of God's work in transformation.

REFLECTIONS AND MEDITATIONS
The leader and participant sit quietly, not too close to each other. Read the meditation passages aloud and follow each with silence.

> **Leader:** "Ask and it will be given you; search, and you will find; knock, and the door will be opened for you" (Matt. 7:7).

[*silence*]

> **Participant:** I once heard a woman say that as an alcoholic, a part of her will always be deeply attracted to alcohol, which seemed a very simple way of putting it, and very true. The attraction—the pull, the hunger, the yearning—doesn't die when you say good-bye to the drink, any more than the pull

toward a bad lover dies when you finally walk out the door. Alcoholism is a disease of relapse and I understand that no single force—not meetings, not willpower, not prayer or guidance or simple wanting—can guarantee that I won't slide back into the relationship, in exactly the same way one slides back into a destructive romance.

Caroline Knapp[13]

[*silence*]

Leader: You [O God] show me the path of life.
In your presence there is fullness of joy.

Ps. 16:11

[*silence*]

Participant: I have been thinking about words of Jesus in Matthew 11:28—"Come to me, all you that are weary and are carrying heavy burdens and I will give you rest." According to these words of Jesus, I can still come to him even if I can't quite let go of all the things that make me so heavy laden. According to Jesus, I can let him hold these things for a little while, long enough to get a rest, even if, for now, I can't quite give them up. And according to this Divine Impossible God, the one who is all I really need, God will always keep God's promises to me, even if I am not so reliable in mine.

Violet Cucciniello Little[14]

Leader: Ho, everyone who thirsts, come to the waters;
and you that have no money, come, buy and eat!
Come, buy wine and milk
without money and without price.
Why do you spend your money for that which is not bread,
and your labor for that which does not satisfy?
Listen carefully to me, and eat what is good,
and delight yourselves in rich food.
Incline your ear, and come to me;
listen, so that you may live.

Isa. 55:1–3

[*silence*]

Participant: I am thankful for the enduring and everlasting mercy, light
and love in my life. . . .
I know I am surrounded by unconditional love, so I am
never alone. . . .
I am protected
I am guided
I am loved
I am Thankful.

Iyanla Vanzant[15]

[*silence*]

Leader: "Therefore, since we are surrounded by so great a cloud of
witnesses, let us also lay aside every weight and the sin that
clings so closely, and let us run with perseverance the race
that is set before us, looking to Jesus . . ." (Heb. 12:1–2).

[*silence*]

The leader and participant may sing a song together.

HYMN SUGGESTIONS

"I Will Do a New Thing in You"
"Breathe on Me, Breath of God"
"How Firm a Foundation"
"Come, My Way, My Truth, My Life"
"The Blood Shall Never Lose Its Power" (". . . gives me strength from
day to day . . .")
"This Is the Day"
"Great Is Thy Faithfulness" (". . . morning by morning new mercies I
see . . .")
"In the Name of Jesus/Victory Is Mine"
"Changed Mah Name"

NAMING THE SLIP ALOUD

Leader: [*Name of person who slipped*], would you please say what
brings you to this time of prayer?

Participant: [*responds with reason*]

Leader: What is your heart speaking as you reflect on this group of readings?

Participant: [*responds*]

Leader: What makes it hard for you to begin again?

Participant: [*responds*]

[*silence for reflection*]

Leader: Let us now place this slip from recovery, and all our frailties, before the throne of grace. Hear these words from the apostle Paul

> I can will what is right, but I cannot do it. For I do not do the good I want, but the evil I do not want is what I do. (Rom. 7:18–19)

> Gracious God, we come before you this day conscious of our frailty, longing for a new beginning. [*Or name other aspects of the participant's experience.*] [*Name,*] would you like to speak aloud your desire for a new beginning?

Participant: [*speaks about desire to move back into recovery, or may take a few moments for silent prayer.*]

Leader: We know God's Word for us to be both judgment and mercy. You have felt the judgment already because of your slip. Now hear the gift of God's mercy offered to you this day:

> The thought of my affliction . . .
>   is wormwood and gall!
> My soul continually thinks of it
>   and is bowed down within me.
> But this I call to mind,
>   and therefore I have hope:

> The steadfast love of the LORD never ceases,
>> [God's] mercies never come to an end;
> they are new every morning;
>> great is your faithfulness. (Lam. 3:19–23)

RECOMMITMENT

Leader: [*Name*], you have named your slip out loud. We have reflected together on the old life of addiction and the new life of recovery. We have heard, together, about the mercy of God, offered new each morning. Are you ready to begin again with this new day of recovery? If so answer, "I do, and I ask God to help and guide me."

Participant: I do, and I ask God to help and guide me.

If the one who slipped earlier took a new name as a sign of his recovery, recall that name now with these words. If the person has not taken a new name, but wants to now, insert the naming ceremony (from pp. 101–4) here.

Leader: Like God's presence with you, your recovery name doesn't disappear when you slip off the path of recovery. Like God, your name stays with you on good days and bad. Let us remember together why you chose the recovery name that you did and what it meant to you at the time of its choosing.

Participant: [*Speaks about the name and its meaning.*]

Leader: [*Given name of person who has slipped*], when you entered recovery [*Or: as you re-enter recovery*], *you chose/you now choose* this name [*Name*] as a sign of your new life. I now call you by name: [*given name and recovery name*]. Remember that wherever you go, this name is a sign that God goes with you.

Using a bit of scented oil, anoint the participant's forehead, making the sign of the cross, speaking these words:

Leader: Almighty God, who has planted in you the seed of desire for new life, graciously grant you the courage, the strength, and the patience to live into your new life.

Participant: Amen.

Leader: Let us go forth in peace, in the name of Jesus.

Participant: Amen.

ᚱᚱᚱᚱᚱᚱᚱ

CELEBRATING THE GIFT OF RECOVERY IN A CONGREGATION

Rejoice with those who rejoice.
Rom. 12:15

Recovery is a gift not only for the addict but also for the communities to which she or he belongs. When someone in a congregation is in recovery, the congregation also receives strength and hope from that person's healing. This prayer expresses the community's gratitude to God for the gift of recovery, especially for the recovery of *this one.* It also serves to give hope to those who are still struggling with addiction but have not yet been able to step into recovery.

This prayer may be used to mark a recovery anniversary and is also appropriate at other times the recovering person might request it. Once the pattern is established in a congregation of offering recovery anniversary prayers, worshipers will sometimes ask for the prayer also for themselves. Some people prefer not to make public the anniversary, or indeed even their life in recovery. Where they do allow their experience to be known, however, public recognition and celebration can be edifying for the whole congregation.

Recovering people are often quite anxious in the weeks and days leading up to an anniversary of sobriety. They often also struggle against pride that can undermine their work in recovery. For these reasons, the anniversary prayer emphasizes God's grace in the gift of recovery rather than the recovering person's own work in recovery. It is best to offer the prayer of thanksgiving on the worship day following the anniversary, when the anniversary is safely past, rather than the one preceding it.

ᚱᚱᚱᚱᚱᚱᚱ

CONGREGATIONAL ANNIVERSARY PRAYER

The prayer below may be noted in the church bulletin or lifted up in the church's prayers, as appropriate. Pastors can use the occasion of a recovery anniversary to offer additional prayers for all who struggle with addiction and in thanksgiving for the gifts of recovery that their congregation experiences in this or other recovering people (for example, honesty, integrity, courage, kindness, patience).

Leader: O God of power and might, we bless you for the liberation of your children from every kind of bondage. Especially this day, we praise you for your work in [*Name's*] life, for releasing *him/her* from the bondage to addiction [*add the nature of his/her addiction, if desired*]. This week, by the grace of God, [*Name*] celebrates *her/his* [*number of years or months*] anniversary of sobriety [*Or: of clean time, or of being in recovery*]: Bless we the Lord.

All: **Thanks be to God.**

FOR FURTHER READING

Margaret Bullitt-Jonas. *Holy Hunger: A Woman's Journey from Food Addiction to Spiritual Fulfillment*. New York: Vintage Books (Random House, Inc.), 1998.

Patrick Carnes, PhD. *Don't Call It Love: Recovery from Sexual Addiction*. New York: Bantam Books, 1991.

Hazeldon: alcohol and drug treatment programs, publishing, research, and professional education. www.Hazeldon.org.

Caroline Knapp. *Drinking: A Love Story*. New York: Bantam Doubleday Dell Publishing Group, Inc., 1996.

Gerald G. May, MD. *Addiction and Grace*. San Francisco: HarperSanFrancisco, 1988.

James B. Nelson. *Thirst: God and the Alcoholic Experience*. Louisville, KY: Westminster John Knox Press, 2004.

Iyanla Vanzant. *Tapping the Power Within: A Path to Self-Empowerment for Black Women*. New York: Harlem River Press, 1992.

Chapter 6

Rituals of Blessing in the Presence of Death

Jesus did not come
to explain away suffering
or to remove it.
He came to fill it
with his presence.
                    Paul Claudel

*C*reating worship experiences in times of loss, whether for a "standard" funeral service or for a loss in pregnancy, the sudden loss of a job, or any other serious loss, provides valuable opportunities to communicate the richness of the Christian faith. Those who plan and lead such ritual occasions may want to dedicate extra time to their preparation, consciously anticipating them as opportunities for Christian witness through worship. Leaders prepare by listening both to the needs of participants and to the depth and variety of Christian worship traditions that might speak to their needs. Exercises found in chapter 7, particularly the ones about using a concordance to find Scripture passages and about choosing appropriate music, will help readers who want to explore in greater depth.

This chapter includes rituals for often-overlooked deaths, like losses in pregnancy and abortion. It also includes a ritual for use at the bedside of a loved one near the time of death, one to use at the grave as a family makes peace with a loved one who has died, and rituals for deaths-in-life: preparation for surgery to remove a breast because of cancer and a ritual for the family of an Alzheimer's patient who, although alive, is also in many ways gone.

More than any other experience, except perhaps the birth of a child, death and other significant losses bring people back to church. People of many faiths and of no faith enter the doors of our churches on these occasions. Some come searching, consciously or not, for something lost in themselves, or for something that could speak to their emptiness. Tend the connections between people's needs as they grieve and the resources of Christian tradition that point them to a living God who will be with them even in the valley of the shadow of death. Then your ministry will open in new ways to people who have stepped away from the church or have never known Christian faith.

LOSSES IN PREGNANCY

For I am about to create new heavens
    and a new earth;
the former things shall not be remembered
    or come to mind.

. . . .

for I am about to create Jerusalem as a joy,
    and its people as a delight.

. . . .

No more shall there be in it
    an infant that lives but a few days.
                    Isa. 65:17, 18, 20

A woman in her seventies was on a nationally televised talk show. When the host asked her about her children, first she named the one that had been still-born more than forty years earlier. There was an awkward pause while the host found words to respond to her unusual sharing. Some experiences mark us deeply, though often they are tucked away in silence. Yet for some they remain a burning hole, unresolved grief, even when they also have live, healthy children.

Mma Ramotswe, a character in Alexander McCall Smith's novels, was visited sometimes with the memory of her child, her loss. When she thought about letting go, a memory came to her about herself with her baby: "She laid the tiny body of their premature baby, so fragile, so light, into the earth and . . . looked up at the sky and wanted to say something to God, but couldn't because her throat was blocked with sobs and no words, nothing, would come."[1] Such anguish to be greeted by death where we had hoped and prayed for life! Can there be a word from God for us in this emptiness?

Silence often surrounds those who experience earlier pregnancy losses, too. These early deaths are particularly hard for us to face, for in childbearing we are vulnerable; there are no guaranteed outcomes. Standing nearby, we often do not know what to say. Many in their childbearing years find it especially hard to face their friends' and loved ones' losses, for those losses remind them of their own vulnerability. Parents and other older family members also find it quite difficult to watch their grown children in such distress. Many do not know how to respond. Relatives also grieve the loss of a grandchild, for instance. Some kind of public ritual, even if small in scope and setting, addresses these various needs.

In many church communities, it is now common practice to offer a full funeral or graveside service, if parents desire it, for a stillborn child. In that case, the suggestions in this ritual could help to shape the funeral, with Scripture readings especially chosen to mention pregnancy, the grief of unexpected losses, and the compassion of God. Many parents of stillborn children have found the public naming ceremony that is the heart of this rite to be especially helpful in their grief.

The losses associated with miscarriage tend to be less visible. Some who miscarry have not yet shared the news of the pregnancy. Many people reacting to the news of a miscarriage assume that grief grows in proportion to the length of the pregnancy, thus often dismissing the feelings expressed as grief. Studies reveal, however, that there is no such hierarchy of grief. Many who miscarry experience the same kind of grief as parents of stillborn children and of children who die soon after birth. Sadness, insomnia, trouble focusing, and guilt feelings are common experiences.

The worship materials offered in this rite are designed as a public marking of grief. The rubrics before the rite show its flexibility: It can be used like a funeral in church; a simpler version could be used at bedside in the hospital with just a few others present. A rite with or without the naming ceremony might take place in the couple's home. The rite might also be used as the basis for a group memorial service, similar to the one for survivors of homicide in chapter 4 (pp. 65–72).

Even when we have no words to speak while suffering losses in pregnancy ourselves or standing nearby, there is a word from God for us. The naming rite in the following ritual speaks of the uniqueness of this child's life—even though it was lost in a miscarriage or stillbirth. In awe, Psalm 139 reminds us that *God* has created us. Isaiah 65 tells us that God's intention for life is that it be full—God is not about calling our babies into heaven to make angels!

One further note: a helpful part of the ritualizing that happens at the time of miscarriage and stillbirth could begin before any particular loss occurs. Congregational worship leaders might include "those who have experienced a loss in pregnancy" in the prayers of the church on an ordinary Sunday, for example. Naming "those who still wait for a child" in the prayers consciously includes in the circle of community couples struggling with infertility and those who have experienced losses. Pastors and worship leaders will often not know who these people are; these small signs can open the door for conversation among members of a church or between members and their pastor.

If our church communities can find ways to be more public about losses in pregnancy, as it is appropriate, then together we can find ways to surround with care those who experience them and can help them to remember and, in Christ, be healed.

❧❧❧❧❧❧❧

REMEMBRANCE AND COMMENDATION
OF A STILLBORN CHILD
OR AFTER A MISCARRIAGE*
by Janet S. Peterman

The core of this worship experience consists of a few simple elements: the Psalm Litany, Words of Comfort, a Scripture reading, and prayers. In its simplest form, it is brief and may be used at bedside in the hospital immediately following the loss, or later in the parents' home.

The public naming of the child may also be used with this simple form, even if only one other is present and even if the loss is an early miscarriage. Ask the parents if naming this child or pregnancy would be meaningful to them. If the gender is not known, the parents may choose a name that may be used with either a boy or a girl, like Kelly, or Jean/Gene.

Alternately, the worship leader may suggest a fuller version of the rite to the parents, like what is printed out below, and together they can decide on the scope of the service, appropriate lessons and music, where to hold the service, and whether others might be invited. Some parents will want no one else and will want to keep the loss to themselves; others will find the presence of family, friends, and/or members of the congregation to be a source of comfort in their time of loss.

The rite may be used as a memorial service for more than one family's loss.

*Janet S. Peterman © 1987. 230 Winona St., Philadelphia, PA 19144. jsp100@verizon.net. Originally published as "Remembrance and Commendation: A Rite to Speak to Losses in Pregnancy," *Lutheran Partners,* July–August 1988, 21–24.

Allow some parents who would participate to choose, with worship leaders, where to hold the service and what selections within the service to use. The approaching Christmas holidays are often a time when grief is especially difficult. All Saints' Day remembrances suggest another possibility. The families' experiences or congregational practice may suggest other possible dates. Plan to use the ritual with time for fellowship or a shared meal.

A stillbirth or miscarriage takes place in the context of a couple's own history. Repeated losses and long struggles to become pregnant intensify grief, as do other medical complications. Worship leaders may add particular concerns like these to the prayers near the close of the service.

Men and women can grieve quite differently with pregnancy losses. Early on, men often experience the loss as a disappointment of what they hoped would be, whereas women often experience it as a death of a life that already was. Allow each parent to express preferences for what they want in the worship experience, as they are able. Often fathers are overlooked when sympathy is extended, especially with miscarriage. They can feel like powerless spectators of the crisis and its medical response. Fathers may welcome the opportunity to take a spoken role in the service, reading a lesson or offering a prayer.

PRAYER OF CONSOLATION

> **Leader:** God of mercy, God of consolation, in our emptiness we turn to You for comfort. Deal graciously with us. Give us the joy of Your saving help as we face death where we hoped and prayed for new life. We ask in Jesus' name. **Amen.**

PSALM LITANY

The psalm is pointed for singing. Alternatively, it may simply be read aloud by one person or read responsively between leader and participants.

> **Leader:** Search me out, O God, and know my heart;*
> try me and know my restless thoughts.
>
> **All:** **Search me out, O God, and know my heart;***
> **try me and know my restless thoughts.**
>
> **Leader:** Lord, you have searched me out and known me;*
> you know my sitting down and my rising up;
> you discern my thoughts from afar.

You trace my journeys and my resting-places*
  and are acquainted with all my ways.
Indeed, there is not a word on my lips,*
  but you, O Lord, know it altogether.
You press upon me behind and before*
  and lay your hand upon me.
Such knowledge is too wonderful for me;*
  it is so high that I cannot attain to it.
Where can I go then from your Spirit?*
  Where can I flee from your presence?

All: Search me out, O God, and know my heart;*
  try me and know my restless thoughts.

Leader: If I climb up to heaven, you are there;*
  if I make the grave my bed, you are there also.
If I take the wings of the morning*
  and dwell in the uttermost parts of the sea,
even there your hand will lead me*
  and your right hand hold me fast.
If I say, "Surely the darkness will cover me,*
  and the light around me turn to night,"
darkness is not dark to you; the night is as bright as
    the day;*
  darkness and light to you are both alike.
For you yourself created my inmost parts;*
  you knit me together in my mother's womb.

All: Search me out, O God, and know my heart;*
  try me and know my restless thoughts.

Leader: I will thank you because I am marvelously made;*
  your works are wonderful, and I know it well.
My body was not hidden from you,*
  while I was being made in secret
  and woven in the depths of the earth.
Your eyes beheld my limbs, yet unfinished in the womb;
  all of them were written in your book;*
  they were fashioned day by day,
  when as yet there was none of them.

All: Search me out, O God, and know my heart;*
try me and know my restless thoughts.²

WORDS OF COMFORT

Leader: The Lord spoke through the prophet Isaiah saying,

"For behold, I create new heavens and a new earth;
and the former things shall not be remembered
   or come into mind.
But be glad and rejoice for ever
   in that which I create;
for behold, I create Jerusalem a rejoicing,
   and her people a joy.

. . . .
No more shall there be in it
an infant that lives but a few days."

(Isaiah 65:17–18, 20, RSV)

In that day, when God creates the new heavens and a new earth, we will not need to gather to mourn the loss of a child. But on this day, we come with sadness to seek the comfort of God. We mourn the loss of a child known to the mother who carried it, to the father who generated it, and to us in hopes and dreams.

All: **O Holy Spirit, Comforter, be present with us.**

A hymn may be sung.

HYMN SUGGESTIONS

"Precious Lord, Take My Hand"
"My Hope Is Built on Nothing Less"
"O God, Our Help in Ages Past"
"Jesus, Savior, Pilot Me"
"Nobody Knows the Trouble I See"
"A Cradling Song" by John Bell

NAMING THE CHILD
The parents may publicly name their child, if they so choose.

A Cradling Song

JENNIFER   11.10.11.4

John Bell

Very tenderly

1. We can - not care for you the way we want - ed,
2. We can - not watch you grow - ing in - to child - hood
3. We can - not know the pain or the po - ten - tial
4. So through the mess of an - ger, grief and tired - ness,
5. Lord, in your arms which cra - dle all cre - a - tion

Or cra - dle you or lis - ten for your cry;
And find a new u - nique-ness ev - ery day;
Which pass - ing years would sum - mon or re - veal;
Through ten - sions which are not yet rec - on - ciled,
We rest and place our ba - by be - yond death,

But, sep - a - ra - ted as we are by si - lence,
But spe - cial as you would have been a - mong us,
But for that true ful - fil - ment Je - sus prom - ised
We give to God the wor - ship of our sor - row
Be - liev - ing that *she* now, a - live in heav - en,

♩ = 70

Text and Music: © 1996, Wild Goose Resource Group, Iona Community, Scotland. GIA Publications, Inc., exclusive North American agent. All rights reserved. Used by permission.

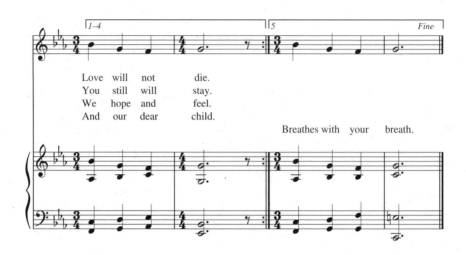

Love   will   not   die.
You   still   will   stay.
We   hope   and   feel.
And   our   dear   child.

Breathes with   your   breath.

Leader: The word of the LORD came to Jeremiah saying, "Before I formed you in the womb I knew you" (Jer. 1:5). The name "Jesus" was given to God's only child to be a sign of salvation and the means by which we may know and remember God's loving-kindness and mercy. We name this child today so that we may remember *her/his* coming among us, and we ask God to bless our remembering.

[*To the parents*]: What will you name this child?

Parents: We name *her/him/this child* [*Given name*]. *(The parents may also mention the significance of the chosen name.)*

Leader: O Child whom we have barely known, we call you [*Given name*]. Receive this name as a sign of your uniqueness to us and before God. We will remember you by this name.

One or more lessons and/or psalms are read. Traditional funeral lessons, psalms, and hymns also fit with this service.

SUGGESTIONS FOR SCRIPTURE READINGS: Deut. 33:27a (KJV); Isa. 40:27–31; Jer. 31:15; Luke 18:15–17; Rom. 8:26–27; 1 John 3:1–2.

A brief sermon or homily may be preached.

A hymn may be sung.

HYMN SUGGESTIONS

"Give Me Jesus"
"Balm in Gilead"
"When Peace, like a River, Attendeth My Way"
"There's a Wideness in God's Mercy"
"Children of the Heavenly Father"

The Apostles' Creed may be said.

Prayers are said in thanksgiving for God's love for the child, as well as for the parents and for all who mourn.

Leader: Eternal God, source of life: We praise you for the gift of life itself. We thank you for the life of this child who has passed among us so briefly, and for your love for this child. (*Alternately: We thank you for this pregnancy, for the spark of life, even as we grieve its unexpected ending.*) Bless we the Lord:

All: Thanks be to God.

Leader: Almighty God, we come before your throne of grace, bold to ask for your healing for [*Name parents. Name other children in the family, grandparents or other family members, if appropriate.*], and for all who mourn. Surround them with your love to sustain them in these days of their loss. O God, in your mercy:

All: Hear our prayer.

Leader: Hear now the prayers of our hearts, offered silently or aloud:

(*Keep silence to allow participants to raise prayer petitions. If the prayers are all silent, leave at least a minute before closing the petition. Whether anyone has spoken aloud, conclude this petition in this way:*) O God in your mercy:

All: Hear our prayer.

Leader: Into your hands, gracious God, we commend all for whom we pray, trusting in your mercy through Jesus Christ, our Savior.

All: Amen.

When Holy Communion is celebrated, it is inserted here, and the service continues with the Peace. The commendation then follows the communion. When there is no communion, the service continues with the Lord's Prayer before closing with the commendation.

BLESSING AND COMMENDATION

Leader: O Child [*Or name*], we entrust you to God who created you. May you return to the One who formed us out of the dust of the earth.

All: Amen.

Leader: Merciful Creator, your Holy Spirit intercedes for us even when we do not know how to pray. Send your Spirit now to comfort us in these days of need and loss, and help us to commend [*Name/This child/This pregnancy*] to your merciful care; through Jesus Christ our Savior.

All: Amen.

Leader: May this child [*Or: Given name*] and all the departed, through the mercy of God, rest in peace.

All: Amen.

Leader: Let us go forth in peace.

All: In the name of Christ. Amen.

෨෨෨෨෨෨෨

HEALING AFTER ABORTION

[Speaking to the crowd, Jesus said,] "Let anyone
among you who is without sin be the first
to throw a stone at her."

John 8:7

The choice of abortion is often hidden, for it can stir up terribly conflicted feelings, even beyond the conflict the decision itself usually engenders. Choosing abortion does not necessarily make grief less real or potent.[3] Unresolved grief can linger in subtle ways, often without a name, and can be triggered by a later event.

Many years after she terminated a pregnancy, the woman for whom this ritual was prepared was expecting the arrival of another child. She became aware of her need for healing from her earlier decision. The woman came seeking renewal and new life. She hoped for forgiveness, cleansing, and healing. She wanted to say goodbye to the child who did not come to birth in order to welcome a new adoptive child more completely. She was seeking reconciliation with God, with the child she had aborted, and with her own deepest self.

When they gathered, it was just three of them: the woman, one of her close friends, and the minister they asked to guide her through the process. They gathered in the darkened chapel of her home church. The mood was quiet and contemplative. They allowed the woman to take the time she needed to speak her needs (to cry, to express her regret, to ask forgiveness, to be cleansed) and to signal when she was ready to move on. The water reminded them of the womb, of cleansing, and of rebirth.

A range of emotions is connected with abortion, varying greatly from woman to woman. Some women feel mainly relief at a burden lifted, for instance, while others feel primarily a sense of loss. If a woman is feeling loss and the loss is new, planting seeds or potting a new plant doesn't work as the symbolic action in this kind of ritual. When the intensity of grief is great, it is simply not the right time to plan for new beginnings. Ministers who want resources for grief to use around the time of an abortion might select from some of the readings and prayers in the miscarriage and stillbirth rite in this chapter. But feelings shift and change over time. Planting seeds can work later, sometimes even years later, especially in this kind of ritual context. Here the ritual provides the opportunity for the woman to name her need for a new beginning, for cleansing and forgiveness. Then planting seeds or a young plant become symbols of new life following forgiveness.

A RITUAL OF CLEANSING AND RENEWAL
FOLLOWING AN ABORTION*
by Susan Cole

This ritual is designed for use after some time has passed from the abortion itself. It addresses not the raw, burning pain of this week's loss, nor the aching pain of emptiness a month later. This ritual speaks to the need sometimes expressed in pastoral conversation for confession and forgiveness, for reflection and for closure that could happen months or years later.

Allow the woman to choose who may be present with her. Though most ritual suggestions around abortion are for the woman alone, it is useful to imagine settings where both partners might participate and to offer the opportunity, where appropriate.

Have a bowl available, a pitcher of water, and a planting pot with soil and seeds. Choose a space conducive to reflection where you will not be interrupted.

Leader: [*holding up the pitcher of water*] Holy One, you who are with us in all things and in every moment, you are deeply familiar with water. Before anything was, you gave form to the seas; you made your home in the deeps as well as in the mist. You piloted Noah to safety through angry waters, and you led the Hebrews through the sea to new life. You were with Jesus in the waters of his baptism in the Jordan, and you were with everyone—indeed, each one of us—when we were in our mothers' wombs.

Today we are present to this water—this water that symbolizes the water of life and the water of the womb—this water that also symbolizes the life wasted, the waters of the womb spent, the tears shed. Be present, O God, with [*Name of woman*] as she pours this water, pouring also her tears and the troubles of her spirit. Be present in and through the water.

*Susan Cole © 1986. Originally published in *Wisdom's Feast: Sophia in Study and Celebration* (Chicago: Sheed & Ward, 1986), 123–25.

Woman: [*pouring a little water from the pitcher as she completes each phrase*]

> I shed tears for . . .
> I am sorry for . . .
> I confess . . .

Others present may take turns completing the sentences and pouring water into the bowl.

Leader: [*holding the bowl of water*] This bowl of water is not poured out in vain; here is water that cleanses, water that heals, water that brings new life. [*Name of woman*], this water is poured out for you. (*The leader and others sprinkle water from the bowl on the woman seeking healing, offering statements of cleansing and healing.*)

> Be cleansed of . . .
> Be healed of . . .

Leader: [*Name*], in and through the One who formed the waters, who is the Water of Life, who was present with you in your mother's womb, you are forgiven.

The leader holds the bowl full of water, saying, [*Name*], this water will now also be poured out for the relationship you are about to begin with your new child. May this water, which cleanses and renews you, nourish the beginnings of your life together.

The woman sprinkles water from the bowl onto a newly planted pot, offering hopes for her new life with her new child. Others may join her, adding their hopes as well.

> I hope for . . .
> May our life grow in . . .

Leader: Holy One, you take life away and you bring new life into being. We ask your blessing on [*Name*] and her child as they begin this new life, this new family. May the tears and the pain of [*Name*] for the child who never knew life bring cleansing and healing; may the tears add their blessing to this new child, and may they open [*Name*] and her child to love and joy and fullness of life.

All: Amen.

They walk outside, following the leader, to a lawn or plot of earth. The leader holds the bowl containing whatever water remains.

Leader: The bitter tears, the mistakes of the past, which are held in this bowl, have been forgiven, and they have been offered as a means of cleansing and new life. Now is the time to let go of them and the past to which they belong, to get ready for the new life that awaits you. Take this water, and pour it out, let it go.

Woman: [*as she pours*]
    Goodbye to . . .
    I let go of . . .

Leader: Life spent leads to new life. The water returns to the earth. It rises once more as the mist. It comes again as the rain. May the One who is present in life, in death, and in rebirth, may the One who sends the rain again and again be with you always.

All: Amen.

❧❧❧❧❧❧❧

LOSING A BODY PART

O Christ, the healer, we have come
To pray for health, to plead for friends.
How can we fail to be restored
When reached by love that never ends?[4]
    Fred Pratt Green

It is always crisis or disaster that brings someone to the place where he or she needs to decide for surgery to remove a part of the body: diabetes out of control; a lump that turns out to be cancer; gangrene; a tragic accident. In the moment there is often precious little time. But if there can be a quiet space, a preparation time, some find it helpful to be given "permission" in the press of other "urgent things," to consider what is ultimate: the gift of life itself; the impending loss and its meaning; the power of God to heal; the support of loved ones.

This rite was designed for use by someone about to have a mastectomy. Its form is less traditional than many of the other materials in this book. Prayers, music, and time for meditation allow the one facing surgery to acknowledge loss and fear and to be open to resources of faith and community for healing. We do not all face the same procedure with the same need. In the case of breast cancer, for example, some will prefer a rite more focused on the grace of finding the cancer early enough for a cure and/or for the blessings of reconstructive surgery. See chapter 7 for suggestions on how to adapt this breast rite to the loss of other body parts (pp. 181–83).

Crisis and disaster leave little time to prepare one's self emotionally and spiritually for surgery. Surgery itself can cause radical shifts in a person's life. In these circumstances even an hour of prayer, silence, readings, and meditation may provide the gift of time and space in which to place one's self in God's hands.

క్షిక్షిక్షిక్షి

PREPARATION FOR SURGERY
TO REMOVE A BREAST
for Mary

Some who will want to use this rite would be too shy to do so with their pastor, especially if the pastor is male. Pastoral conversation about impending breast surgery, however, could well include discussion about the rite. Have a copy printed out to give to her and discuss with her how she might make time among many competing demands for this kind of spiritual preparation. Consider with her who might share the meditation time with her—a prayer partner, spiritual director, minister, or close friend (hereafter noted as "prayer partner"). Though the meditations and prayers might be read through alone, it is better done with another, better to have another give voice to hope and reassurance when she does not feel it. Who could best assist? Is there someone who could lead singing?

If she does it alone, let her read and sing silently or aloud.

Let the breast that is about to be removed be seen and appreciated. If it feels appropriate, sit bare breasted during the rite, or with a loose fitting blouse open at the front. Photograph the naked breast. These suggestions highlight the need for comfort and privacy where there will be no interruptions. If the one facing surgery craves the presence of a few friends, she may then prefer to cover her breasts.

She may wish her husband or partner to be present. Partners have losses, too, with a loved one's surgery and need support. The ritual could work with the couple together, or it might not. Partners' needs are often quite different in this moment.

Silence is woven in between the readings. Allow enough time that you do not need to rush. Each meditation is meant for pondering before moving on to the next one. The experience might well take a couple of hours.

If a minister is the prayer partner and the woman desires it, they might share Holy Communion. Use music or silence as it is most fitting.

Originally this rite was printed out and set up in a blank book journal. Each reading, song, and prayer was put on a page by itself to encourage silence for meditation as part of the reflection time or for written reflections. Empty pages remained for pictures or for later journal writing.

SILENT MEDITATIONS
Use each reading one at a time, followed by silence. The prayer partner may read each aloud, or the woman or others who attend may take turns reading. Share insights from the reflection times, as appropriate.

Meditation

You grew up and became tall
and arrived at full womanhood;
your breasts were formed,
and your hair had grown;
yet you were naked and bare.
Ezek. 16:7

[silence]

Meditation

[My surgeon] told me some women preferred a mastectomy. Weeks of radiation would then be avoided, along with side effects. I'd just get it over in one fell swoop.

Sure. Just get your breast cut off and it's all over. Permit me to doubt. I'm rather attached to my breasts—downright fond of them. They're part of my identity as a woman and an important part of my sexual pleasure.

Cathy Hitchcock[5]

[*silence*]

Meditation

Joseph is a fruitful bough,
  a fruitful bough by a spring;
  his branches run over the wall.
The archers fiercely attacked him;
  they shot at him and pressed him hard.
Yet his bow remained taut,
  and his arms were made agile
by the hands of the Mighty One of Jacob,
  by the name of the Shepherd, the Rock of Israel,
by the God of your father, who will help you,
  by the Almighty who will bless you
  with blessings of heaven above,
blessings of the deep that lies beneath,
  blessings of the breasts and of the womb.

Gen. 49:22–25

[*silence*]

Meditation

I was told by two doctors, one female and one male, that I would have to have breast surgery, and that there was a 60 to 80 percent chance that the tumor was malignant. Between the telling and the actual surgery, there was a three-week period of the agony of an involuntary reorganization of my entire life. . . . within those three weeks, I was forced to look upon myself and my living with a harsh and urgent clarity that has left me still shaken but much stronger.

Audre Lorde*

[*silence*]

Meditation

Jesus, Savior, pilot me
Over life's tempestuous sea;
Unknown waves before me roll,
Hiding rock and treach'rous shoal;

*Reprinted with permission. *Sister Outsider: Essays and Speeches,* by Audre Lourd. Copyright © 1984 by Audre Lourd, Ten Speed Press, Berkeley, CA. www.tenspeed.com

Chart and compass come from thee.
Jesus, Savior, pilot me.

As a mother stills her child,
Thou canst hush the ocean wild;
Boist'rous waves obey thy will
When thou say'st to them: "Be still."
Wondrous sov'reign of the sea,
Jesus, Savior, pilot me.

When at last I near the shore,
And the fearful breakers roar
Twixt me and the peaceful rest,
Then, while leaning on thy breast,
May I hear thee say to me:
"Fear not, I will pilot thee."

Edward Hopper[6]

[*silence*]

Meditation

How fair and pleasant you are,
　　O loved one, delectable maiden!
You are stately as a palm tree,
　　and your breasts are like its clusters.
I say I will climb the palm tree
　　and lay hold of its branches.
O may your breasts be like clusters of the vine,
　　and the scent of your breath like apples,
and your kisses like the best wine
　　that goes down smoothly,
　　gliding over lips and teeth.

Song of Solomon 7:6–9

[*silence*]

Meditation

Making love. Nursing a baby. Holding a child. Hugging a friend.
Standing in a bathing suit at the pool.
It's my life with others that I have such trouble imagining
if I were to be without a breast.

Janet Peterman

[*silence*]

Meditation

And when [the doctor] touched the area, I felt my flatness.[7]

Judy Hart

[*silence*]

Meditation

Every loss is a death.

[*silence*]

Meditation

The prayer partner reads the following introduction, then the questions in italics. Leave silence before moving on to the remainder of the reading.

Judy Hart practiced a focusing technique to get through panic attacks after she was first diagnosed with breast cancer. She started by going to a comfortable spot, a porch overlooking geraniums and out onto the ocean. She sat with an empty chair beside her and invited her terror to sit beside her.

Can you invite the loss of your breast to sit beside you? To sit with the loss fully, not avoiding it, not laying it aside?

[*silence*]

(Some of Hart's thoughts:)

Just now I've stopped writing and allowed my tears to flow, tears of sadness, loss, inexorableness. All I've built hasn't been enough to prevent this from happening. . . . I couldn't prevent this. . . .

How are you now, my terror? I reach my hand out to you. You seem to have put your feet up on the railing, and together we can stare out over the sand to the sea and wonder about something that is larger and more spiritual than what I have felt negatively engulfing me. We will cope as we are already coping because we don't have to encompass everything at once—just whatever is going on now. And we can feel the love we have for ourselves and others and the love others have for us.

Judy Hart[8]

[*silence*]

NAMING THE LOSS

The one facing surgery speaks aloud to the prayer partner, naming the losses she is feeling. If she is alone, she takes time to reflect on her losses.

People close to the one facing surgery feel a sense of loss, too, though theirs is of a different character. Others who are present may wish also to share and may do so if it doesn't shift the focus too much from the one facing surgery.

SONG

Rocka My Soul (Traditional Spiritual)
Refrain: Rocka my soul in the bosom of Abraham
Rocka my soul in the bosom of Abraham
Rocka my soul in the bosom of Abraham
Oh, rocka my soul.

So high, can't go over it
So low, can't go under it
So wide, can't go 'round it
Got to go through the door: **Repeat Refrain**

PRAYERS FOR THE SURGERY AND FOR HEALING

Prayer
Partner: For all who feel the need for healing, of body, mind and spirit: Christ, in your mercy:

All: Hear our prayer.

Prayer
Partner: For [*Name the one facing surgery*] in these days of preparation and waiting: Christ, in your mercy:

All: Hear our prayer.

Prayer
Partner: For other loved ones, especially [*Names as appropriate*], that you, O Lord, may bring healing and ease the pain: Christ, in your mercy:

All: Hear our prayer.

Prayer
Partner: For [*Name the husband/partner and children of the one*

having surgery], and for all who wait and fear and touch and hope: Christ, in your mercy:

All: Hear our prayer.

Prayer
Partner: For those who have traveled this path before; for those who stand beside and listen: Bless we the LORD:

All: Thanks be to God.

Prayer
Partner: For nurses and doctors, that their skill and compassion may bring healing to [*Name*]: Christ, in your mercy:

All: Hear our prayer.

Prayer
Partner: For these things and for all that You see that we need:

[*Silence, or other petitions . . .*]

Prayer
Partner: Into your hands, O loving Savior, we commend all for whom we pray, trusting in your mercy.

All: Amen.

WORDS OF REASSURANCE
The prayer partner reads these aloud, or they take turns reading. Leave silence between readings.

Prayer
Partner: God is our refuge and strength,
a very present help in trouble.
Therefore we will not fear, though the earth should change,
though the mountains shake in the heart of the sea;
though its waters roar and foam,
though the mountains tremble with its tumult.
There is a river whose streams make glad the city of God,
the holy habitation of the Most High.
God is in the midst of the city; it shall not be moved;
God will help it when the morning dawns.

The nations are in an uproar, the kingdoms totter;
[God] utters his voice, the earth melts.
The LORD of hosts is with us; the God of Jacob is
our refuge.

Ps. 46:1–7

[*silence*]

Without breasts
a woman's heart
rounds and
softens her
body
bears her milk . . .
Elana Klugman[9]

[*silence*]

Rejoice with Jerusalem, and be glad for her,
all you who love her;
rejoice with her in joy,
all you who mourn over her—
that you may nurse and be satisfied
from her consoling breast;
that you may drink deeply with delight
from her glorious bosom.

Isa. 66:10–11

[*silence*]

I will accompany myself in this voyage into the unknown. . . .
I will remember the life-saving reasons for this. . . .
I will honor all that I am.

Judy Hart[10]

[*silence*]

So we do not lose heart. Even though our outer nature is wasting away,
our inner nature is being renewed day by day. . . .

For we know that if the earthly tent we live in is destroyed, we have a
building from God, a house not made with hands, eternal in the heavens.

2 Cor. 4:16; 5:1

Participants sing a song or hymn, or listen to music together.

HYMN SUGGESTIONS

"O God, Our Help in Ages Past"
"O Christ, the Healer, We Have Come"
"How Firm a Foundation"
"The Lord Is My Light"
"Oh, Let the Son of God Enfold You"
"There Is a Balm in Gilead"
"Precious Lord, Take My Hand"
"When the Storms of Life Are Raging"

STANDING WITH OUR LOVED ONES IN THEIR DYING

Swing low, sweet chariot, comin' for to carry me home.
Swing low, sweet chariot, comin' for to carry me home.
Traditional Spiritual

Brenda and Barbara knew how to use their last precious bit of time with their father. They spent it with him as he had long ago taught them when he took them to church with him—by turning to God in prayer and song. They sat on either side of him, held onto him, prayed with him, and sang their favorite hymns, including this end-of-worship hymn:

Savior, again to thy dear Name we raise,
with one accord our parting hymn of praise;
once more we bless thee ere our worship cease,
then, lowly bending, wait thy word of peace.[11]

It was holy time, filled with awe. They knew that God was with them as their father crossed over from this life to the next.

Advances in medical technology, the return to dying at home with the support of hospice care, and longer life expectancies have all contributed to a shift in our experiences of our loved ones' deaths. Many more North Americans are dying at home again, or in the hospital after the removal of life support. Thus there are now many opportunities for family members and close friends to be present at the moment of death.

Ministers and chaplains sometimes share these final moments with families, but more often they are not there. And many people in our churches are no longer as steeped in Christian faith traditions as Brenda and Barbara are, nor, often, do they feel secure taking on spiritual leadership at bedside. Pastors can assist their people to bring their own resources of faith to their loved one's final hours. Prepare these worship materials in printed form in advance. Make them generally available in a fellowship hall or chapel, for instance, or offer them to the families whose loved one's death draws near. Having suggestions in hand will give many what they need to stand confidently in faith with their loved ones at the hour of death.

When we sit with our loved ones as they die, the experience may be new to us, but we already have available to us years of experience of living with each other. How we spend these moments together will reflect the patterns and experiences of our living. Whether conscious of our spiritual practices or not, each of us has some of the tools we need to minister to our loved ones as they die.

Lillie was a Christian worker who shaped the life of her home and family around Christ. She led daily family devotions. As loved ones came and went, traveling far from their East St. Louis home, before each one would leave, she gathered them all for a prayer circle. Together they prayed that the one about to set off for a journey be granted traveling mercies. The rituals of Lillie's life became the rituals of her death.

When Lillie's daughter, Valerie, came for what would be her last visit, she saw her mother's suffering and knew that it was her time. She promised her mother that she would remember and use all that her mother had taught her. She gave her mother permission to let go. She found strength to walk through their last hours with her mother because together they focused on God.

They spent hours together over two days. There was no pretending that she wasn't dying, but the hours were anything but somber. Lillie's loved ones told her what she meant to them. They told her stories of their earlier experiences with her, laughing through their tears. Through their sharing, they showed her that she had not lived her life in vain. They read Scripture to Lillie, choosing from her favorites and reading passages that reminded them of her. They sang favorite hymns. They used Reiki, a touch technique; they wiped her tears and her mouth; they held her hands.

In the end, they formed a prayer circle around her, loved ones touching her, grounded together in the love of God and in the presence of each other. Together they prayed for traveling mercies for Lillie's crossing over. It felt, Valerie said, like midwifery: dying to them, but being born into a new life, into eternity, for her.

The rubrics in the Crossing Over ritual offer family members some ways to prepare themselves as death draws near. It provides an order of service with various options and allows loved ones, if they desire it, to choose readings and songs that express their faith. Then perhaps they will also experience the life of God, even in the midst of death, and they will know, with the apostle Paul, that whether we live or whether we die, we are the Lord's (Rom. 14:8).

ᚙᚙᚙᚙᚙᚙᚙ

CROSSING OVER:
RITUAL AT THE HOUR OF DEATH
remembering Harry and Lillie

Some people seem to want to be alone at the moment of death. Even if family and friends are nearby for the final few days, some people will appear to wait for a moment when everyone is out of the room to die. Prepare to use these resources near the time of death and perhaps you will also be present for the moment of death itself. This choice may not be in your hands.

Consider how universal these elements of ritual are at the hour of death: circling around the dying one, touch, sacred speech, song, stories, prayer. If you ponder the life of the dying one near you, you will know which words are sacred; which readings, songs, and prayers fit for this one's dying. The character and nature of the dying person shape the dying. If you feel stuck in imagining, ask your minister or someone else to sit with you who knows both the dying one and the resources of Scripture and Christian worship traditions. Work through each of the suggested sections below in advance, if you are able, to prepare yourself for the final hours.

If death comes more quickly than you had imagined, or if a number of people gather for a final worship time together at bedside, you may not have hours of time to sit together. Choose one lesson, a prayer, and a benediction. Add a song or a time for participants to speak to their loved one if that seems appropriate. Use the fuller version of the rite offered below for a longer sitting time, as a kind of vigil.

At the end of life, some people are on a ventilator for their breathing, making it impossible for them to speak. Even so, that does not mean the dying one is not participating with you. Some will mouth the words of songs as others sing or nod their heads or squeeze a hand. You will sometimes not know for sure if your loved one can hear you, but the sense of hearing is one of the last things to go. Speak with the hope that your loved one may hear you, even if she or he is unresponsive. If a loved one is no longer conscious, touch can still connect you.

Be conscious of the limits of the patient's surroundings. If the dying one has a roommate in the hospital, for instance, ask the nursing staff to assist you in setting up the room with the other patient in mind. Stand or sit around the dying person so that you are able to touch his or her arms, legs, or head, as appropriate.

If a minister or other lay leader from the congregation is available, he or she may serve as the leader. If not, let the people gathered choose who can carry that role.

GATHERING
The leader lights a candle as she or he begins, if the setting allows it.

> **Leader:** We have come to be with you in this hour, [*Name*], confident that in our dying, as in our living, we are the Lord's. The peace of the Lord be with you.

> **All: And also with you.**

SHARING STORIES
Those gathered share stories of their life with their loved one. The sharing time can be ordered and led by one of the participants or be less formal and stretch over a long time. Leave periods of silence and allow crying or other expressions of emotion to arise and fall as they will.

> **Leader:** You are invited to share a story with [*Name*] and with us, some experience that you cherish, something that speaks of *his/her* character or strength, something that makes you laugh.

(Leave silence, enough for all to share who want to share. When they are finished, close with these words:)

> **Leader:** [*addressing the one dying*] [*Name*], we give thanks to God for you, and for the life we have shared. Know that we will carry you with us after you are gone. We see your suffering. When you are ready, we want you to know that we are not holding you here: You may go.

> **All: The God of peace go with you.**

Someone or all gathered may sing a song.

HYMN SUGGESTIONS

"Abide with Me"
"All Praise to Thee, My God, This Night" (verses 1–3, 5)
"Now the Day Is Over"
"Just as I Am"
"O Love, That Will Not Let Me Go"
"Rock of Ages"
"Even as We Live Each Day"
"My Faith Looks Up to Thee"
"Come, My Way, My Truth, My Life"
"Open Our Eyes, Lord"
"Oh, Let the Son of God Enfold You"
"Pass Me Not, O Gentle Savior"
"The Blood That Jesus Shed for Me"
"Sweet Hour of Prayer"
"Jesus Loves Me"
"Jesus, Remember Me"

This period of Scripture readings can stretch over time, with silence between readings. One or more lessons may be read in succession. Choose readings that have been important to the one dying, or that speak to his/her character, that are beloved by those gathered, or that fit the season.

SUGGESTIONS FOR SCRIPTURE READINGS: Job 19:23–27a; Pss. 4; 23; 31:5; 46; 91; 116, esp. vv. 15; 121; 130; 139:1–18; Isa. 40:27–31; 43:1–4a; Rom. 8:26; 8:31–35, 37–39; 14:7–8; 1 Cor. 13; Luke 2:25–32; John 14:1–7; Phil. 1:3; 1 Thess. 4:13–14; Rev. 21:1–4.

Participants may reflect on the readings aloud or in silence, if they so desire.

PRAYER

Leader: Oh, Lord, our Lord, how majestic is your name in all the
earth! You held Noah and his family safe through forty days
of storm and flood. You led your people Israel by a pillar of
cloud by day and a pillar of fire by night. You sustained
Jesus through the wilderness, in temptation, in sorrow, in
suffering, and through death. Grant your healing presence
to our *sister/brother* [*Name*] as *she/he* returns to you. Ease
her/his transition from this life. Make *her/his* way peaceful.
We ask in Jesus' name.

All: Amen.

Someone or all gathered may sing a song.

HYMN SUGGESTIONS

"When Jesus Wept"
"There's a Sweet, Sweet Spirit in This Place"
"Blessed Assurance"
"Where He Leads Me"
"When Peace, like a River"
"Leaning on the Everlasting Arms"

BENEDICTION

Leader: The LORD bless you and keep you. The LORD make His face to shine upon you and be gracious to you. The LORD lift up His countenance upon you, and give you peace.

All: Amen.

PRAYER IN THE MOMENTS FOLLOWING DEATH

Begin by keeping silence after the last breath, for as long as seems fitting. Then the leader offers this commendation and prayer.

Leader: Into Your hands, Gracious God, we commend [*Name*]. Receive *him/her* into the arms of your mercy. We ask in Jesus' name.

All: Amen.

Leader: Eternal God, in whom we live and move and have our being, we thank You for this sacred time together. One more time, we thank you for [*Name's*] life. As you have sustained [*Name*] through *her/his* illness and dying, so sustain us now, we ask you, in this time of our sorrow and loss. We ask in Jesus' name.

All: Amen.

GRIEVING DEATH IN LIFE

Can a woman forget her nursing child,
  or show no compassion for the child of her womb?
Even these may forget,
  yet I will not forget you [says the LORD].

                                        Isa. 49:15

There isn't one way to die. We die young and old, peacefully and violently, surrounded by loved ones and alone. When we speak of dying, we are usually referring to the end of our physical bodies. But there are other deaths. The death that comes with Alzheimer's disease, for example, is different from many others. It comes in stages.

Many loved ones have a hard time articulating their anguish. I remember a conversation with a man whose wife had just died of Alzheimer's. The last year or two she had been cared for in a nursing home. He visited her there often even though he found being with her difficult. She would lash out especially at him, and he could hardly bear it. "I lost her long ago," he bemoaned. "Now I am just exhausted from the burden of her care, from the burden of watching her in this state for years." He wished he had been able to have a funeral for his wife years before, when he had really lost the woman he loved, the mother of his children. But when would that have been?

There is often little space for family members of people afflicted with Alzheimer's to acknowledge what is lost along the way. It was this man's request echoing in my ears while I watched another woman care for her mother with Alzheimer's in her home that led me to plan this gathering.

The purpose of such a gathering is threefold. First, it enacts a family truth: we are facing this ongoing loss—together. Second, it is a public acknowledgment of grief and loss. It provides a context in which a family can grieve even though the person is still physically alive. It allows family members to find words for the varieties of their experiences of loss. Third, the gathering also allows the family to marshal its strength together to walk their loved one home, however long that shall take, and to support the daily work of the primary caregiver(s).

I encountered an unusual but beautiful request at a funeral. After the funeral director closed the casket, the woman's closest family prepared to join the procession to the grave. Nancy, the daughter who was the spokesperson for the family, pulled the funeral director aside. "When we get to the cemetery," she said, "when we're a ways off from the grave, I want the procession to stop and let me out. I want to walk beside my mother. I don't want her to have to make her final journey alone."

The funeral director turned to his assistants and asked them to identify a place in the cemetery's maze of roads where they could stop the automobile procession and let Nancy out to walk with the hearse to her mother's grave. At the appointed spot, when Nancy got out, so did everyone else. The whole family walked behind the hearse: and Elizabeth was accompanied to her grave surrounded by the ones who loved her most.[12]

Caring for a loved one with a disease like Alzheimer's brings peculiar challenges for a family, often stretching on for years. When that path is especially difficult, this ritual helps a family articulate their commitment and support to walk their loved one all the way home, together, in both grief and hope.

෯෯෯෯෯෯

GATHERING OF THE FAMILY OF A LOVED ONE WITH ALZHEIMER'S DISEASE
for Mary

For this particular gathering to work, the patient must have lost the capacity to understand ordinary conversation. Otherwise the conversation about the person in her/his presence would be inappropriate. Families of patients with other kinds of brain injuries or dementia might also benefit from such a gathering. Choose a time of day and a setting where the person with Alzheimer's will be comfortable.

When would one have such a gathering? You might decide to tie the occasion to an outward sign of physical decline—for example, the point at which one's mother can no longer walk unassisted to the car. She might still be carried out to the doctor in her wheelchair, but her isolation is surely heightened with this kind of physical decline. Others experience the decline more in terms of their loved one's mental losses, especially the loss of meaningful conversation, or the loss of mutual recognition, or loss of memories of the life they shared. These moments, however, are harder to mark on the calendar and can be points of intense family disagreement. Families might therefore better choose a time for this ritual related to a favorite holiday or gathering time, full of its own traditions and memories, when they might naturally come together anyway. Plan the gathering so that as many family members and close friends can be present as possible, yet without so many that the space becomes overcrowded or chaotic.

Have someone lead the gathering who is not a family member.

Prepare in advance: have one or two people who are especially close to the primary caregiver(s) help prepare a list of things others might do to help with the person's ongoing care. Primary caregivers often have a hard time naming the kinds of assistance that would truly be helpful to them and yet are often overwhelmed by unrelenting tasks. The list might include meals brought in, help getting the person to the doctor, or sitting time with the person so that the caregiver can get out for church or other activities. Have someone other than the primary caregiver take on the role of coordinating helpers, in consultation with the caregiver.

Suggest that participants bring pictures from their loved one's life. Other tangible signs of the person's strengths—physical reminders such as plants, handwork, or signs of the person's life work or interests—are also helpful. If there are favorite hymns or Scripture texts, participants may also bring these.

The gathering may be set in a service of Holy Communion, if it is appropriate to this family. A meal or other refreshments might end the time together and allow the sharing of family members to continue more informally.

GATHERING

Place photographs and other signs of the person's life on a table in the center of the seating space or on small tables near those gathered. Encourage people to look through the pictures as they wait for others to arrive.

The leader briefly introduces the gathering:

Leader: I've heard it more than once: At the funeral of someone with Alzheimer's, someone in the family says, "But we lost him years ago. We should have had the funeral then." [*Name ways that the person with Alzheimer's is still present to his/her family; for instance: If you see Frances with a baby, see her eyes light up, or watch her with an ice cream cone, you know that she is still very much with us.*] But there have been tremendous losses along the way, losses we want to be able to speak out loud, together.

[*Name's*] care is also much more difficult now. By this gathering, we want to pledge our support to [*Name primary caregiver(s)*], who *care(s)* for *her mother* day in and day out. We ask God's blessing on the ways that each one here supports [*Caregiver(s)' Name(s)*] with *her mother's* care.

These or other brief readings, perhaps favorites of members of the family, are read.

Answer me when I call, O God of my right!
    You gave me room when I was in distress.
    Be gracious to me, and hear my prayer. (Ps. 4:1)

". . . indeed [God] is not far from each one of us. For 'In him we live and move and have our being.'" (Acts 17:27–28)

Leader: Let us pray. By your presence, O God, make of this circle in which we sit sacred space: wide enough for each of us to come as we are; spacious enough to hold our sorrows; generous enough to offer each of us a place of rest in Your everlasting arms.

We bless you, heavenly Father, for the life of this family. For [*Names of loved ones who have died*], for [*Name of person with Alzheimer's, with a description of his/her place in the family: for instance, "mother and grandmother"*], for their children [*Names*], for [*Name other significant relationships of people gathered: for instance, "For grandchildren, loved ones and friends who gather with them"*]: Be their strength, their rock, the light upon their path. We ask in Jesus' name. **Amen.**

SHARING
The leader leads those present in sharing about their loved one, with these or similar words.

Leader: As we gathered today, we were looking at pictures of [*Name's*] life and of the life of this family across the years. As you look at these pictures, can you put into words what you have lost with [*Name*] in the last few years? What did you have that you no longer have? What do you miss?

Allow enough time for everyone who wants to share. Leave some silence, as it is needed, to allow the more hesitant ones to come to voice. When there has been enough time for sharing, lead prayer.

Leader: Let us pray. Gracious God, we remember before you this day [*Name's*] life that has slipped from us because of Alzheimer's. We thank you for giving *her/him* to us to know and to love. For what is now gone from *her/him*: comfort us who mourn these losses. Surround us with your loving presence that we may know that you carry us still. We ask in Jesus' name. **Amen.**

The leader assists those present to offer themselves in the care of their loved one.

Leader: The fourth commandment says, "Honor your father and your mother, so that your days may be long in the land that the LORD your God is giving you" (Exod. 20:12). [*Caregiver's name*] has said that *she* would like to honor *her* *mother* in these days of *her* life by caring for *her* at home. We want to use this time together to offer ourselves to help with [*Name person with Alzheimer's*] care. Our ways of giving are many and various, but it is a human need to give of ourselves to those we love. Each of us has parts of ourselves that we want and need to give to [*Patient's Name*] on her long walk home. Along the way, we also hope we can be helpful to [*Name of primary caregiver(s)*] in *her* daily care of *her mother*.

Name a few examples of how individuals present are offering themselves as part of the patient's care. Allow time for others to name what they might offer. When participants have spoken, someone close to the caregiver(s) raises other possibilities from their advance preparation and the conversation continues. When all have finished, close with prayer.

Leader: Let us pray. The apostle Paul reminds us that there are varieties of gifts, but they all come from the same Spirit. And there are varieties of service, but they all come from the same Lord (1 Cor. 12:4–11). Gracious God, we ask that You bless each one here in his or her giving, whether the gift is from near or far, that they may all rejoice in the strength and power that You, O God, have given them to show forth Your love. **Amen.**

Close with a hymn.

"There's a Sweet, Sweet Spirit in This Place"
"I'm So Glad Jesus Lifted Me"
"Bind Us Together, Lord"
"Leaning on the Everlasting Arms"
"Somebody Prayed for Me"
"Abide with Me"
"What Wondrous Love Is This"
"Come, Thou Fount of Every Blessing".

All gathered share a meal together.

GOING BACK TO THE GRAVE

In Jewish tradition, *Yahrzeit*, the first anniversary of a death, signals the time for a graveside service to place a headstone. Christian tradition most often passes over the anniversaries of deaths in silence. I have often wished for more of a communal sense of mourners' first year of grief. An experience with one family made me wish, as well, for a return trip to the graveyard as a regular part of our congregation's ministry.

The graveside ritual included here helps family members name the ways that their loved one blesses them, even after death. The placing of a headstone might call forth this ritual. It could also be used at the anniversary of a death, at a birthday, or at another significant date. The needs of family and friends who will gather will clarify the right time. In the absence of a community standard like Jewish tradition provides, congregations may want to develop their own practice of offering this ritual at the one-year anniversary of a death.

I first went back to the grave with a family of ten children, some by a second father after the first one died. When I knew them, they were more contentious than many families, especially after their mother died. None of the children belonged to our congregation, but the mother and father/stepfather had belonged in the last years of their lives. They died within a few years of each other, first the mother, then the father. I found the preparation of the father's funeral especially difficult because of the family tensions.

But at just the right time, in God's time, one of the daughters called and asked me to be with the family to say prayers at the cemetery after they had placed the headstone. It had been six years since their mother died, and more than two, their father. A brother had recently died and now it was the right time. They had some music in mind that they wanted to play. They wanted me to lead a service.

That day it was hot and humid. Almost everyone was there under a tree in a beautiful old cemetery: children, grandchildren, and great-grandchildren, including two newborns. They stood together in the shade.

What made this experience different from the funeral? Lucille and Edgar had wanted their children to know unity. In the months after Edgar's death, in various ways, their children longed for the presence of their parents. It wasn't articulated in just this way, and they still clustered together in smaller groupings under the tree. But they came, together. After the service, they ate a meal at one son's house, together.

It is often at the funeral that loved ones are able to grasp for the first time—really grasp—that someone they love has died. Sometimes it takes years after that to incorporate the meaning of that person's life, and death, into one's own life.

In West African tradition, when people gather for a special occasion, they often begin with a pouring of libation. As water is poured, those gathered call forth the names of the ancestors who have gone before them who still shape and support the lives of the living. With humility and honor and gratitude, the people call out the names of their ancestors. Whether we call them "Daddy and Mommy" or "our ancestors," we find an anchor for our lives through our ongoing connection with our loved ones who have died.

※※※※※※※

ANNIVERSARY SERVICE AT THE GRAVE
in memory of Lucille and Edgar

Choose as worship leader someone from outside the family.

Advance planning includes conversation with the family about location, possible music, readings, and readers. If appropriate to location and season, planting flowers might be added to the opening of the gathering. Flowers might also be planted beforehand to prepare the space. Some public parks may require advance permission to hold a gathering there or to plant flowers.

Music serves as a cohesive force for the experience at the grave. In this ritual, the family brought a portable CD player and some popular gospel and rap songs that had been meaningful to them in their grief. Find music the group will be able to sing together or will appreciate together as they listen. If there is no common experience of hymn singing, bring a portable CD player; popular gospel, rap, or inspirational songs might be helpful for some families in their grief.

Not everyone grieves in the same way. Even among siblings, each child's relationship with a parent is unique. This ritual allows space for participants to express their feelings and to name their own experiences. Leave sufficient silence to allow the more hesitant in the group to find their voices.

The ritual is completed when the group gathers together for a meal after the time at the grave. Sharing a meal together can draw participants to each other.

GATHERING
Gather at the grave itself. If there is no gravesite, or if ashes were dispersed at sea or elsewhere, gather at an appropriate place nearby such as on a boat, at the shoreline, or in a park.

To signal the start of the ritual, sing a hymn or play some favorite music, live or recorded. If the group will plant flowers as part of the ritual, provide for more music and do the planting while the music plays.

MUSIC SUGGESTIONS

Hymns:
"For All the Saints"
"Precious Lord, Take My Hand"
"Here I Am, Lord"
"He Hideth My Soul"
Recorded:

"Great Is Your Mercy"	D. McClurkin [gospel][13]
"I Wish"	R. Kelly [rap]
"Fields of Gold"	E. Cassidy [popular]
"How Lovely Is Thy Dwelling Place"	J. Brahms [classical]
"Lord's Prayer"	A. H. Mallotte

NAMING THE BLESSINGS
As the music finishes, the leader encourages participants to name the blessings of the one(s) who have died.

> **Leader:** In Genesis, the first book of the Bible, we find the story of Israel's patriarchs, Abraham, Isaac, and Jacob. As each one dies, he (for these stories do focus on the patriarchs, not the

matriarchs) gathers his children to him and blesses them. These blessings are not simple farewell speeches but a bestowal of power. The old, dying one names something that he grants to his son, and by saying it, it is so. So Isaac blessed his son Jacob, and Jacob his son Joseph (Gen. 27:1–29; 48:1–22; 49:1–28).

Since [*Name(s)*] *has/have* died, we have had a chance to reflect on *his/her/their lives* and what *he/she/they* mean to us. It takes longer than the week of the funeral to be able to name the blessings *he/she/they* have given us, knowingly and unknowingly, with *his/her/their lives*. We gather today at *this grave/resting place* to name those blessings and to thank God for [*Name'(s)*] life and memory.

Keep silence until people name the blessings as they have experienced them. The leader may set the tone by naming one such blessing, as appropriate.

When all who want to speak have finished, the leader offers a prayer:

Leader: [*Name(s)*], we thank God for you, for the memory of you, for the ways you stay with us still.

All: Amen.

Participants may share readings or poems, if they desire to do so.

The leader or other reader from the family or church reads one or two short readings from Scripture. Choose from among texts usually read at a grave-side committal service, or other passages that are appropriate.

SUGGESTIONS FOR SCRIPTURE READINGS: Job 19:25–27; Pss. 23; 46:1–3, 10–11; 90:1–6; 118:5; 121; 133; 146:1–7; Isa. 40:6–8; Rom. 14:7–9; John 11:25–26a; John 14:1–3; Rev. 21:1–4.

CLOSING
The leader prays an improvisational prayer touching on the themes expressed by participants in their sharing, followed by the Lord's Prayer. Alternatively, the leader may encourage participants to share their own prayers or may use this prayer:

Leader: Eternal God, God of Abraham and Sarah and of every generation, we give you honor and glory for the life of this family. We give you thanks that in your abundant mercy you have given [*Name(s)*] to us. Especially do we praise you for *his/her/their* gifts of [*Name some of the qualities mentioned by the group in their sharing*]. Bless this family that mourns *his/her/their* passing, holding them together in blessed memory. We ask these things in Jesus' name, who taught us to pray:

All: Our Father. . . . Amen.

The ritual concludes with music, sung or recorded, and a benediction.

MUSIC SUGGESTIONS

Hymns:
"Thy Word Is a Lamp unto My Feet"
"God Be with You"
"I'm So Glad Jesus Lifted Me"
"When Peace, like a River"
"Bind Us Together, Lord"
"Leaning on the Everlasting Arms"
"Abide with Me"
"The King of Love My Shepherd Is"
"Children of the Heavenly Father"
Recorded:

"Stand"[14]	Donnie McClurkin [gospel]
"I Need You to Survive"[15]	Hezekiah Walker & the Love Fellowship Choir [gospel]
"You Raise Me Up"[16]	Josh Groban [popular]

Leader: Now may the God of peace, who brought back from the dead our Lord Jesus, the great shepherd of the sheep, by the blood of the eternal covenant, make you complete in everything good so that you may do his will, working among you that which is pleasing in his sight, through Jesus Christ, to whom be the glory forever and ever (Heb. 13:20–21).

All: Amen.

Allow time for participants to view the new headstone and/or nearby stones, as appropriate, before moving on to a common meal.

FOR FURTHER READING

About Losses in Pregnancy

Sherokee Ilse. *Empty Arms: Coping with Miscarriage, Stillbirth and Infant Death*. Maple Plain, MN: Wintergreen Press, 1990.

Kim Kluger-Bell. *Unspeakable Losses: Understanding the Experience of Pregnancy Loss, Miscarriage, and Abortion*. New York: W. W. Norton & Company, 1998.

Christine O'Keeffe Lafser. *An Empty Cradle, a Full Heart: Reflections for Mothers and Fathers after Miscarriage, Stillbirth, or Infant Death*. Chicago: Loyola Press, 1998.

Ava Torre-Bueno. *Peace after Abortion*. 2nd ed. San Diego, CA: Pimpernel Press, 1997.

About Dying

Maggie Callanan and Patricia Kelley. *Final Gifts: Understanding the Special Awareness, Needs, and Communications of the Dying*. New York: Bantam Books, 1992.

Joyce Hutchinson and Joyce Rupp. *May I Walk You Home? Courage and Comfort for Caregivers of the Very Ill*. Notre Dame, IN: Ave Maria Press, 1999.

About Grief and Healing

Susan Talia de Lone. *Love, Loss and Healing: A Woman's Guide to Transforming Grief*. Portland, OR: SIBYL Publications, 1998.

C. S. Lewis. *A Grief Observed*. New York: Harper & Row, 1961.

Martin E. Marty. *A Cry of Absence: Reflections for the Winter of the Heart*. San Francisco: Harper & Row, Publishers, 1983.

Froma Walsh and Monica McGoldrick, editors. *Living Beyond Loss: Death in the Family*. New York: W. W. Norton & Company, Inc., 2004, 1991.

Nicholas Wolterstorff. *Lament for a Son*. Grand Rapids: Wm. B. Eerdmans Publishing Co., 1987.

About Ritualizing at the Time of Death

Jeanne Daly McIntee. *To Comfort and To Honor: A Guide to Personalizing Rituals for the Passing of a Loved One*. Minneapolis: Augsburg Fortress, 1998.

Sarah York. *Remembering Well: Rituals for Celebrating Life and Mourning Death*. San Francisco: Jossey-Bass, 2000.

PART THREE

CREATING NEW RITUALS
FOR CHRISTIAN WORSHIP

Chapter 7

Creating New Worship Materials

Remove the sandals from your feet,
for the place on which you are standing
is holy ground.

Exod. 3:5

*I*n chapters 3 through 6, we explored a variety of new rituals, worship experiences that arose in many different ways. The Lenten praise service with the residents of our church's transitional housing program, for instance, arose by thinking about a kind of structure that could hold the women's testimony about God's carrying them through years of living on the street. The breast rite developed as I thought about what kind of readings and silence could help a friend carve out some quiet time to ponder life and healing in the harried days between the decision to remove her breast for cancer and the day of the surgery. Marguerite Sexton knew she needed to be at the spot in the parking lot where a woman had been killed. Reclaiming that place for life centered her thinking about the new ritual she created. There isn't one right way to create new worship materials, nor even one right way or place to begin.

Yet it is also true that much of what is offered for new worship materials in our time doesn't work very well, or lacks emotional depth, or uses language that falls flat. Thus the reflections and exercises in this chapter are offered as a kind of tutorial in the process of creating a new ritual. Follow them in consecutive order, and they will walk you through a process of creation. Together they make up a whole, carrying you through a series of reflections, from the recognition of a need that might be addressed through ritual to the kinds of texts and music that will speak to the need and to symbols that will embody God's response to the need and a structure to hold it together.

Each of the reflections, and each of the exercises contained within them, can also stand alone. In a moment of pressing need, reflecting on ways to enhance an existing ritual through more appropriate music or a broader range of biblical texts might provide the right resource to strengthen materials that you have before you. The series together, though, provides a way to step back from the urgent press of ministry and to reflect on possibilities of ritual to address the deeper needs of the people in your ministry. Do this work, and you will strengthen your church's worship life. The reflections ask you to sharpen your skills for worship leadership, especially when you can engage in them or work on them without the expectation of an immediate product. Take time that stretches over days or weeks, and surround your reflection with prayer.

After the tutorial, the chapter concludes with two additional reflections. The first explores how existing rituals might be adapted for new circumstances. The second continues a discussion from the recovery rituals in chapter 5, illustrating how worship leaders and those working in pastoral care can assist someone develop affirmations as a spiritual practice.

The exercises and reflections in this chapter are offered with a prayer that you may discover joy in the work of creating new rituals. Pondering these things and working on them, you will help ritual to do its work—that the people in your place might encounter the presence of a living God; find healing; grieve; celebrate; or be moved on to a new stage of life. And through all these circumstances, even the most difficult, may you and they together discover ways to lift your hearts and voices in praise of God.

A PROCESS FOR CREATING NEW RITUALS

- Name a need to be addressed by a new ritual.
- Find appropriate biblical texts to speak to the need.
- Make connections with existing worship materials.
- Explore the nature of symbols and identify appropriate symbols.
- Consider symbolic action and chart a symbol's movement.
- Consider structure and pull the parts into a whole.
- Consider the role of music in your ritual.

NAME A NEED TO BE ADDRESSED BY A NEW RITUAL

You probably bring with you an idea of a need that you might like to see addressed by ritual, or you wouldn't likely find yourself reading these exercises. But have you listened deeply enough? The first step in creating a new ritual involves listening for, and naming, the need.

Suppose you'd like to create a ritual for a couple who is divorcing. Some couples are able to work with a mediator and come to resolution about the ongoing care of their children, and will feel primarily a deep sadness about the ending of a marriage that was less than they hoped it would be. It might be possible for such a couple to take part in a ritual together, perhaps to enact their intent to share the raising of their children. Many couples, however, will fight so fiercely and experience the ending of their marriage in such divergent ways that a common ritual would be impossible. A divorce ritual might well be a ritual for one partner alone. To prepare an end-of-marriage ritual you would need to listen carefully to the couple you know, to the way they experience the ending of their marriage.

If you want to work through these reflections and exercises as a series, have a specific ministry situation in mind where you believe a new ritual might be helpful, or reflect on a couple you know and the end of their marriage.

Listening Exercise

- Lay a blank sheet of paper before you. Close your eyes if that is helpful. Call the situation to mind and listen: What voices do you hear? How would you name what this person or couple is experiencing?
- When the voices speak clearly in your mind, start writing your thoughts down on the paper until no more come. Stay with your paper 5–10 minutes beyond when you finish writing. Sometimes important insights come after the most obvious thoughts are out of the way.
- Name the need. Review what you have written down. As concretely as you are able, try to name what the person is experiencing. When I thought about a woman who was caring for her mother who had Alzheimer's disease, I heard her grief over her mother's no longer being able to speak. I also realized that the burden of her mother's care was growing much more difficult and that she was feeling overwhelmed by being the primary caregiver.
- Prioritize your observations. Look over all of the needs and experiences you have named on the paper. Which one is the most important at this time? What are the top three? A ritual might well address a few needs, but one or two needs should be the primary focus.
- Before moving on to the next reflection, take time to test out your listening skills with the person you are imagining working with. As an alternative, choose a colleague as a conversation partner, describe the

situation, and ask how he or she hears the need. Such conversations can broaden and deepen the work of creating new worship materials.

In any case, do not hurry on to the other reflections in the series before your reflection in this exercise is complete. This is the foundation of your new ritual. The more specifically you can name the need, the better able you will be to hear how God's Word speaks to that need. Fear and anxiety are similar but not the same experience, nor is loneliness the same as despair. Listen.

FIND APPROPRIATE BIBLICAL TEXTS TO SPEAK TO THE NEED

The second step of ritualizing is to gather appropriate texts and stories from Scripture and Christian tradition. Gather them first, without deciding how to use them. Gather them as a list, or in your heart, until you have more than you will need. It's not time yet to assemble the pieces; there are other considerations before we reach that point. For now, be sure that you cast the net widely enough.

When you hold a particular need clearly in focus as you listen, you will hear a word from God for the one(s) you are considering. After I had baptized the stillborn child, I found myself waking early and hearing voices as I drove on the expressway from one place to another: "But we have *this* to say to her mother! And what about *this?* And there is *this*. . . ." Material for a new ritual for use after miscarriage and stillbirth began to press itself upon me. It came in small pieces: first Scripture texts, then songs, then the idea of naming.

As an example of this phase of gathering materials, here are some of the early pieces that came to me as I thought about the woman whose child was stillborn:

- A text from Isaiah 65, which is an apocalyptic vision about God's new heaven and new earth, which mentions infants that live but a few days.
- Ps. 139:15: "Your eyes [O God] beheld my limbs, yet unfinished in the womb . . . they were fashioned day by day, when as yet there was none of them."[1]
- A prayer in our denomination's funeral service, calling on the God of consolation for comfort.

Held together, the biblical texts and prayer convey that it is not God's will that parents should suffer the death of their little one; God is the author and giver *of life.* This is the word from God that I would try to communicate through the miscarriage and stillbirth ritual I was developing.

Notice that at this stage you are gathering together materials that are familiar to you from other contexts, from other experiences. You may also begin to
associate hymns, songs, and musical pieces that could enhance the ritual.
While music will be discussed more fully below, for now add these musical
insights to your ideas of how God speaks to a need.

When you allow your mind to wander, you may discover associations at
once untraditional, yet also apt. Imagine the poignancy added to a ritual to
prepare for surgery to remove a cancerous breast that cites Gen. 49:25. The
text is describing the patriarch Joseph as one especially blessed by God:
"The Almighty . . . will bless you with blessings of heaven above, blessings
of the deep that lies beneath, blessings of the breasts and of the womb."
Breasts are cherished as a blessing *of God*. In the cherishing, the present loss
is in some small way comprehended.

Step back for a moment and reflect on the range of biblical texts you have
available for use in your new ritual. You can broaden that range by using a
concordance. When Marguerite Sexton prepared her "Blessing Ritual:
Reclaiming a Place of Violence" after a young woman was killed in a hospital parking lot, she alluded in a prayer to the creation story in Genesis 1
and to Old Testament ritual acts of cleansing. When I adapted her ritual for
the murder of a church member's son, I wanted to add Scripture readings.
With keywords "weep," "place," and "wilderness," I found these texts that
might work:

- Jer. 31:15: Rachel weeping for her children
- Gen. 28:16: Jacob at Bethel: "Surely the LORD is in this place—and I
  did not know it!"
- Jer. 31:2: "The people who survived the sword found grace in the
  wilderness."

As I worked through those keywords, these additional texts also came
to mind:

- Ps. 22:1–2: "My God, my God, why have you forsaken me?"
- Isa. 65:20: An apocalyptic text in which God is creating a new heavens and a new earth: "No more shall there be in it an infant that lives
  but a few days, or an old person who does not live out a lifetime."

You'll discover as you write out a list of possible texts that some words and
verses seem to provide a fit better than others do. I chose Rachel's weeping

for her children and Jacob's realizing that God was present when he did not know it. When we used the ritual again at the first anniversary of the man's death, his mother wanted some word about stopping the violence on our streets. Together we found Ezek. 45:9, a word from the Lord about putting away violence.

Now try the exercise yourself. With the need clearly in mind that you isolated in the listening exercise, what keywords might you take to the concordance? And what do you find in Scripture as you wait for a word from God in this situation?

Concordance Exercise

- Find a quiet space. Bring a Bible, a concordance, paper, and pen.
- You are searching for a word to speak to a particular need. Begin with prayer for the leading of the Holy Spirit.
- Think of several keywords related to the situation you've chosen. Find the concordance listing for each word and explore the Bible passages that use each word. Make note of the passages that you want to return to.
- When you have more than enough, review the possibilities and choose a reading or readings to center your ritual.

MAKE CONNECTIONS WITH EXISTING WORSHIP MATERIALS

When I developed a ritual for use after miscarriage, I wanted those who used it to associate the experience with a funeral. Many parents who experience miscarriage report that people around them often downplay their loss, as though it isn't much to mourn. The parents themselves, especially the mother, often experience the miscarriage as a baby who has died. Using a familiar prayer from our denomination's funeral service is one way of helping people to associate the ritual with a funeral, thus presenting the loss as a death to be mourned. Identify associations you'd like to encourage between the situation you are considering for a new ritual and your church's existing rituals and practices.

The process can work both ways. New ritual material can also strengthen existing worship practices. When a woman prepared to join the church after decades away and a move into recovery from addiction, we adapted our congregation's Affirmation of Baptism service, by which people become members. The service takes place in the gathered community, with a person from the church standing with each one joining, which would make concrete the human connections available to this person to support her sobriety. The service also affirms God's loving purpose and support for her and places joining a community of faith within the ongoing struggle between good and evil in the world.

Though our congregation has many people who return to the church after a time away and we always highlight the importance of the experience of joining the church, the weight and significance of the moment of joining for a woman who had been away for decades seemed to get lost. We wondered what this new member might carry away from the service as a living reminder of that moment in her life of faith. Together we came upon choosing a new name. This woman chose "Elizabeth" after the story in Luke 1, for it reminded her of the strength to endure even a very long time of waiting. Taking permission to name herself and choosing her own new name came to have deep significance in this woman's understanding of Christian faith. For her, part of the faith has to do with having the strength to speak for herself in her life, in her work, and in her church.

A new name emphasized the magnitude of the woman's step into recovery, which engendered her move back to church, and it is an ever-present reminder of new life. The action of choosing a name complemented the service that already existed but also enhanced it according to the particular needs of the one returning to church after so long a time away.

Think about possible associations between the ritual you are considering and your tradition's existing rituals and worship practices. Identify prayers, readings, or ritual actions that might be helpful in the ritual you are creating. Peruse your church's worship book, as well as worship books from other Christian traditions, to see if existing materials might enhance the ritual you are preparing.

EXPLORE THE NATURE OF SYMBOLS
AND IDENTIFY APPROPRIATE SYMBOLS

After the Germantown Mennonite Church voted to accept gay men and women into its membership, delegates from fifty-two Mennonite churches in the Philadelphia region voted overwhelmingly to take away the credentials of the church's pastor. The moderator of the regional Mennonite conference brought the news to the congregation.

Without forethought or planning, upon hearing the announcement Ken White, a gay member of the congregation, asked the moderator to escort him to the door of the meeting house and to cast him out. At first the moderator refused, saying she had nothing personal against him. But other members insisted: they wanted conference leaders to see the consequences of their vote. Finally the moderator agreed. She accompanied White to the door saying that she did so as a representative of the 81 percent who had voted to expel.[2] In light of such a strong vote for expulsion, what was it about the symbolic action of showing Mr. White to the door that seemed at first undesirable?

When expulsion was simply written out, words on paper, votes on ballots, a resolution stating church policies and actions, no one who voted to expel had to look at a real gay person and put him out of the circle of fellowship. Acting out the expulsion—representing it symbolically—left no questions about the words' meaning. Here the line is drawn: these people are inside; these are out.

Symbols convey meaning that is deeper than words. Symbols speak to our hearts. They appeal to more than our thinking, cognitive self. A symbol's power comes in a flash of recognition. V. H. Kooy calls a symbol a visual representation of what is unseen or invisible.[3]

Finding Appropriate Symbols

While ritual itself functions symbolically, ritual also needs material objects, signs, and tokens that convey the rite's meanings.

Choosing a symbol means naming or identifying a visible, physical representation of a deeper, less tangible truth. A ring symbolizes love and commitment for *this one*. This candle reminds our family of a baptism and thus of belonging to God. A garden names a grandparent's favorite hobby and so anchors us into our family, even after the grandparent dies.

A symbol works by association. The deeper truth—of love, or commitment, or belonging, or responsibility—is imprinted on our hearts along with the image of the object that calls it to mind for us. They arise together. When I see the photograph I took one August of the sun rising over Assateague Island, or touch a shell from the beach where our family vacations, the peace and joy I experience there become almost palpably present to me.

When an older woman was forced to move into a nursing home, the African violet that was presented to her spoke of her gifts as a gardener, a capacity she carried with her into the nursing home, though physically she was failing in many other ways.

When you look back on a worship experience you have led, whether it "worked" to convey the word from God that you intended will be determined in large measure by whether the symbols and symbolic action you chose fit.

Exercise: Naming Symbols

- Find a quiet place for meditation. Think about your life work, an important relationship, or a place that refreshes your spirit.
- What object(s) symbolize your work, your relationship, or your place of refreshment for you?
- Think about a worship experience that happens regularly in your congregation. What symbols do you notice? What meaning do the symbols convey? Do they work as they are intended, or can you think of others that might work more effectively in that setting?
- Now return to the need for a new ritual that you have been using in the earlier exercises. What might symbolize the need you have isolated? What could symbolize God's response to that need?

Note: If you find this exercise hard, be patient with yourself. Many people have never thought consciously about what symbolizes experiences in their lives. Some find it awkward to begin naming symbols. This exercise offers a place to start. Sometimes the resistance comes from not trusting your own intuition to name what is important.

If you find the exercise difficult, try doing it with someone you trust or a small group of people. As you watch other people name their symbols, you will probably begin to realize what works symbolically for you, or in the ritual you are considering. When you can visualize objects and actions that work symbolically for you, you'll be better able to pay attention to how they function for others and within a ritual.

CONSIDER SYMBOLIC ACTION AND CHART A SYMBOL'S MOVEMENT

Consider the following story as you think about symbolic action.

The book of Jeremiah provides a historical record of the prophet's dire warnings to the people of Israel. When Jeremiah looks at Israel, he sees greed, corruption, and violence—all violations of Israel's covenant with the Lord. Your choices will lead you to ruin, he warns them, and so they do: Babylon overruns Jerusalem. Jerusalem's leaders are carried off into exile. The victors seize her houses, her fields, her riches.

Set against this desolation, Jeremiah hears God instructing him to go out and buy a field. It was worthless land, for now Babylon claimed it all; Israel's ownership meant nothing. With this symbolic action, Jeremiah is saying, You are feeling God's judgment now. But God will not leave you. Let this field stand as a sign: we will return. Let this field stand as a sign: God will not forsake us, even when we have turned away. God will once again bring us home (Jer. 32:1–44).

On one level the land is just the land. It is dirt to walk on, to grow crops in, to build houses on. But on another level, the land is a sign of the people's relationship with God—of the place where they are rooted, where they stand on the promises of God. It is just this possibility of dual meaning that makes symbols so important to the task of ritualizing. When participants or leaders of rituals find the right symbols and symbolic actions to convey the heart of a ritual's meaning, the meaning is seared into participants' consciousness. They will carry the meaning with them long after other details are lost. (Recall the story of Sarah and her parents in chap. 2, pp. 17–18: "Little one, you are marked with the cross of Jesus. You are mine; I will go with you.")

Symbols can also go awry. Reread the story in chapter 2 about Nicholas Wolterstorff's son's funeral (pp. 19–20). No one had foreseen, said Wolterstorff, "the impossible pain" of blowing out the symbol of the resurrection of his son.[4] Symbols carry such weight and power!

The exercise below helps you to imagine ahead of time how a symbol moves through a ritual.

Exercise: Charting a Symbol's Movement

Think for a moment about how wedding rings function at a wedding. The people gather, and the nature of marriage is laid out in Scripture readings and in the marriage service. The couple come to the altar and make their vows to each other. The best man holds up the rings; the pastor blesses them; the man and woman place them on each other's fingers as a sign of love and faithfulness while they say words to that effect. The two wear their rings as the service goes on with God's blessing and prayers.

Now consider another ritual symbol you have witnessed or a symbol you have isolated through reflection. For each symbol, use a time line or a list. Some people prefer to work this kind of thing out in their heads. Track a symbol from its entrance to its exit by means of the following questions.

- What is the symbol? What are other alternatives to this symbol? Why have you chosen this thing and not another?
- When will the symbol be introduced in the ritual?
- By whom?
- What happens next with the symbol?
- When does the symbol cease its role in the ritual?
- How does that happen?

- Does the symbol represent a human need or the word of God speaking to that need?

Complete this exercise by repeating it with more than one symbol.

When you have followed a few symbols through a rite, reconsider the problem Nicholas Wolterstorff experienced at his son's funeral. Can you imagine a more successful way of using the symbol of a resurrection candle within the graveside part of a funeral?

CONSIDER STRUCTURE AND PULL THE PARTS INTO A WHOLE

A need sharply in focus, biblical texts that bring a word from God to speak to that need, and symbols of both the need and God's response: significant component parts of ritual are gathered, yet the ritual is not yet whole. What is missing? We have not yet considered prayer, and some reflections on music follow. But first, let's return to the question of structure.

Read pages 6–11 in chapter 1 to consider the question of a ritual's structure and of how open and closed sections of ritual work. Then, with the need clearly in mind that you have identified, ask yourself these questions as you seek to discover an appropriate structure for the new ritual you are creating.

- Do the pieces you have gathered so far in preparation for this ritual suggest a structure in themselves, as the Lenten praise service did (chap. 1, pp. 7–8) or as the breast rite does (chap. 6, pp. 139–47)?
- What flow suggests itself? Can you see a beginning, a middle, and an end? Place the pieces in a possible order and step back to review the whole. Is there too much? Too little? What's missing? Where might music be helpful? (See below.)
- Which parts of the ritual, as you now see it, are "closed"? Which "open"? As you look at the whole, do you need more open spaces? Is there a place for silence?
- Are there factors in the circumstances you are addressing with this ritual that dictate a time or a place that the ritual should or should not take place? Is the sanctuary appropriate?
- Now consider where and how prayer shall be included. At what points is prayer needed? What kind of prayer will be offered: free prayer; a printed prayer; intercessory prayer? Who might help to lead prayer or other sections of the worship?

CONSIDER THE ROLE OF MUSIC IN YOUR RITUAL

When our congregation gathers for a Tenebrae worship service on Good Friday evening, musical selections—choral and instrumental pieces, solos and congregational singing—constitute such an important part of the service that it is hard to imagine the service at all without music. Music, readings, prayer, and silence, and the move in the sanctuary from light to darkness: these things *are* the worship experience. In many rituals, however, music isn't asked to play such a crucial role. In fact, songs or hymns are sometimes tacked onto the beginning or end of a ritual in a quite perfunctory way. But music is uniquely capable of helping ritual do its work, for, like symbols, it can convey meaning and power more deeply than words.

At its best, music communicates a ritual's meaning in ways that supplement text and prayer. Music also helps to hold ritual together and moves participants through the experience. Consider how music might enhance your worship experiences by thinking about the component parts of music, each in turn.

- Songs convey their meaning in part by their *words*. Hymn texts can support or undermine the meaning of the intended rite. When the young adult steps away from home to be on his or her own for the first time, the African American praise hymn "I Will Do a New Thing in You" works better than the old hymn "Just as I Am." Ask yourself what meaning(s) you would like to convey with a hymn. Do the lyrics help to do that?
- What *style* or *type* of music would work for your situation? Does the situation call forth praise or lament or both? What musical style is comfortable for the people involved? Do they prefer standard Protestant hymns, or folk or gospel songs? What do they know by heart?
- How will the music chosen function within the ritual? Drums and church bells call people to worship. Singing a hymn can help people feel a sense of community with each other or allow someone to express his or her faith. Quiet music in the background can make a space for prayer or meditation. What do you want the music to do for your ritual?
- What is the interplay between the music and other parts of the ritual? Will a song reinforce a Scripture reading? Where might silence balance words and music? How might the movement of the ritual make a place for the praise of God, which is often accomplished best through singing?
- Given the circumstances in which your ritual will take place, identify *who* will be responsible for the music and *how* they will do it. Can a

soloist or leader sing the verses while everyone else joins in on a simpler refrain or antiphon? If so, participants will not need to juggle books and papers and those who cannot read are also included. Will someone play an instrument? Are there musicians who could lead, especially if the music is unfamiliar or if the people who will gather do not know each other well? Who will lead the various musical pieces? Will printed music be needed? Will you need to play a tape or CD to support insecure voices? Could a digital keyboard bring a fuller sound?

Even a cursory review of the reflections and exercises in this tutorial will reveal how time-consuming the process can be if you are starting from scratch, especially if you are new at creating worship materials. Worship leaders do become practiced over time. Often leaders bring expertise in at least one of these reflection areas, and, with the gift for worship leadership, creating new rituals can become second nature. In the end, if you give yourself time to ponder it after the experience is over or discuss it with a colleague, you will know what worked and what didn't. You will feel sustained yourself by the appearance of the Holy Spirit, will feel yourself carried with those gathered, and will find your own lips for praise. To God be the glory.

ADAPTING EXISTING WORSHIP MATERIALS FOR A NEW SETTING

The work of creating new worship materials is often richer when worship leaders build on the work of others. This reflection offers an example of how two chaplains adapted Marguerite Sexton's "Blessing Ritual: Reclaiming a Place of Violence" in chapter 4. Sexton developed the rite following a murder in a domestic dispute. They adapted it for use on a college campus following a rape.

Additional thoughts then follow, as a second example, about how you might adapt the breast rite in chapter 6 to use for other kinds of surgery.

A STUDENT SERVICE OF HEALING

The young woman was alone when the man, dressed as a security guard, entered her dormitory room and raped her. Then he disappeared. This violence struck students at their core. Their fears, their sense of danger, were heightened by the man's deception in dressing like a security guard and by the fact that he was still at large.

The college responded by providing counseling services and by stepping up security, but many students didn't go to the counselors, finding their fear hard to talk about. One of the women who lived near the room on that hallway began to give voice to their need: "Something has to be done," she said. It was as if she were saying, "We need words, but we ourselves also need to take action of some kind. We need to *do* something together."

Laura Ford and Violet Little, chaplains at the college, discovered that none of the worship books they knew provided for an occasion like this, and they realized they would have to create something specific to their situation. But they had heard about Sexton's blessing ritual, so they also knew they would not have to start from scratch. They decided to adapt that rite to their situation. The chaplains wanted to create a worship experience to enhance students' sense of safety, while not making claims about God that were too facile.

In Sexton's ritual (pp. 60–63), consideration of place dominated. The parking lot is a public space. The hospital owns it; what happens there affects many who pass through it, who park their cars there. But no one lives there. A dormitory hallway and dorm rooms are also public spaces but in a profoundly different sense. They belong to the college, but the rooms themselves are also home to the students who live there. When violence intrudes into our most personal spaces, there is nowhere to retreat.

Little and Ford set out to craft a Student Service of Healing for the students of the dorm where the rape happened, who were especially traumatized. They had handed over all the power to define their space to the rapist and referred to the building where they lived as "the place where she was raped." Thus with the worship experience, the chaplains set out both to reclaim the space in God's name and to help students rediscover their own sense of power to define their living space.

Much of the chaplains' discussion in preparation for the healing service centered around the place for their gathering. The room of the crime was not a possibility; it was closed and locked. The dorm itself was one wing of a building; an old community chapel was in the other wing, but the campus had changed hands, and the chapel wasn't used as a chapel anymore. In fact, the sacristy, the preparation room behind the altar, was used to store artwork. Nevertheless, it was still known as an old chapel, and at the chapel's altar, participants would be able to sense the presence of the dorm nearby. Claiming space from the old sacristy to hold their gathering felt, symbolically, like the reclaiming of the dormitory space that they were doing with the ritual itself.

Claiming that love is stronger than evil is an act of faith counter to some human experiences, especially the experience of rape. It is, however, a faith the community can hold for individuals within it, especially when they cannot. The chaplains used the basic framework of Sexton's ritual, the opening Litany of Reclamation, the words of blessing, and the sprinkling of water, and they all stood together in a circle. But keeping the students in mind, they added to the framework to better suit their situation.

It seemed essential to them that the students be given the opportunity to give voice to their concerns and to place them in God's hands, so they made a place in the ritual before the blessing and after the water for students who desired to speak. Fear and anguish were present but were not the final words to be spoken. They prayed using the Psalms, for it was an interfaith service. Then they prayed for the one who was raped and for the other students' safety and protection. They substituted songs that the students liked to sing for the songs in the original rite.

A community's worship has a wider effect than we sometimes see. In the weeks following the healing service, the chaplains heard from the director of the counseling department that even students who had not been at the service spoke of it and found it helpful for their own healing. Some talked about it as a kind of exorcism, of chasing demons away. Worship can help to rebuild the fabric of community.

ADAPTING THE BREAST RITE

The rite "Preparation for Surgery" in chapter 6 contains a series of meditations for a woman to use before a mastectomy. How might such a rite be adapted for use before surgery to remove other body parts, in the aftermath of such surgery, or, more generally, around major surgery of any kind?

Begin by considering the circumstance before you. Generalities are not very helpful. It matters, for example, which body part is involved. Some parts of us, like breasts, are surrounded with modesty or embarrassment that can make open conversation more difficult. Some circumstances are life threatening. Did the required surgery result from an industrial accident? Might there have been negligence involved? Does the age of the person make the circumstances more complicated? What effects might the loss have on the person's ongoing life? Will she or he need to use a wheelchair? Will sexual function be affected? Is the person facing a hysterectomy beyond childbearing age, or might she still be hoping for a child?

When you have pondered the circumstances yourself, then listen as the person talks about what that experience is like *for him or her*. The particular needs and experiences of the person will help to shape the ritual.

Adapting worship materials involves two primary considerations: structure and resources. A rite's structure includes its setting, the flow of its movement from beginning to end, and the balance of the parts of the rite with one another. Resources are the individual parts of the rite, like readings and prayers. First, consider the structure.

In the breast rite, because of the very personal nature of breasts and the crisis of a life-threatening illness, pastors are encouraged to offer the materials to the patient for her use either with a loved one or alone.

The first part of the rite includes ten reflections on breasts and loss and on the threat of cancer and of dying. These reflections are juxtaposed later in the rite with words of reassurance. Throughout, the reflections come from Scripture and contemporary sources. The hymns suggested offer comfort and turn the patient's eyes toward God. The materials are meant to create a time of silence, meditation, and prayer that can take as long as two hours.

Let's consider, as an example, changing the breast rite into a set of meditations and prayers for use with an elderly person who is already hospitalized and is about to lose a foot because of diabetes. How well might the original structure fit the new situation?

The rhythm of the rite translates well—readings, silence, prayers, words of reassurance. Though the modesty of breasts is no longer an issue, the loss of any body part is deeply personal. This kind of ritual doesn't call for a crowd and is appropriate with at most a selected few others present.

What needs adapting? An elderly patient might well lack the stamina for an extended time of meditation; a hospital setting might preclude that much private time. A few meditation selections and one or two words of reassurance might be sufficient. Without the sexually charged attention to breasts, a pastor of either gender could easily lead an adapted rite at hospital bedside the evening before surgery, with or without close family.

Next, review the resources within the original rite with an eye to the new setting. Remove readings, hymns, or prayers that don't fit the new situation and replace with more appropriate pieces.

While the prayers and hymns suggested in the breast rite would work well in many settings, most of the readings would not. Of the ten opening reflections, the first seven refer specifically to breasts or breast cancer in a range of contexts. The last three speak more generally. In the Reassurance section, Psalm 46 and the reading from Judy Hart speak well in other contexts, while the other readings do not.

Decide how many readings you want in each section of the rite. Should you desire more readings or a wider variety of texts, work with a Scripture concordance, perhaps to choose Scripture texts that mention legs or feet, or that give voice to God's blessings of the body, or that acknowledge the pain of loss. For example, in a story in Luke, a woman anoints Jesus and wets his feet with her tears (7:44–46). In John, Jesus washes his disciples' feet with love (13:4–5). These readings could be added to the reflections in the first part of the rite. The prophet Isaiah uses running as an image of the hope and strength that believers find with God, especially when they are discouraged (40:27–31). It might be added to the reassurance texts in the latter part of the rite.

DEVELOPING AFFIRMATIONS
AS A SPIRITUAL PRACTICE

When Roy Oswald developed his affirmations, he began with a conscious purpose: to quell deeply rooted negative thoughts and feelings. His affirmations root him into the life of faith by gathering together pieces of Christian tradition, statements about the meaning of faith, and much positive thinking. Hear a few lines of his "Personal Affirmation":

> My goal this day is total health. . . . The unconscious mind will assist me in eating foods that are healthy and wholesome for me and avoiding those that are destructive to my body. My unconscious mind will assist me in reducing my intake of caffeine, sugar, salt, white flour and high-fat food. . . .
>
> Spiritually I grow each day in profound awareness of my essence, of the Gift of Life, of the truth and reality of what is and the many ways God richly blesses me and others. . . . Everywhere I go I am loved and supported by others. . . .[5]

Oswald's affirmations are densely worded, but he has committed them to memory. He often travels for work, requiring long drives to the airport. He begins to recite his affirmation as he leaves home for the airport and then repeats the series three times, interspersing them with chants that center him. With a core of consistent material, he brings in new material as he needs it, especially as he faces new situations that are difficult or frightening for him.

Oswald's experience shows us several things about the way affirmations function:

- The affirmations address issues that the person finds especially challenging.
- They work best when they incorporate phrases that summarize faith and life experience that are already meaningful.

- Like prayer or other spiritual practices, affirmations do their best work when they can become a regular part of a person's life rhythm.
- They are repetitive but can evolve over time.
- The affirmations' repetition works both on the conscious and unconscious mind.

When committed to memory, reciting affirmations moves the one using them to another level of spiritual practice, freeing him or her for deeper relaxation and meditation. (Unlike Oswald, many people prefer not to be driving when using their affirmations!)

These reflections on helping people develop their own life affirmations grew in my work with people in recovery, for the use of affirmations is common in 12-step programs. Affirmations often become a kind of partner in the work of recovery. They speak of a faith that is alive and active, reminding the recovering person daily, or even hourly, of the presence of the living God. As you read through this process, you'll see its original context, though others, too, can find affirmations helpful—to establish a rhythm for daily life or prayer, to be carried through difficult circumstances, and to remember, in whatever circumstances, that we stand in the presence of God.

As in preparing new rituals more generally, participants who have a role in creating affirmations often discover that the process contributes to their own growth and healing. Developing affirmations is an exercise that some will want to do alone; others will find it impossible without someone else to lead or guide their exploration. The reflection may be led by a pastor, spiritual friend, or spiritual director, one-on-one or in a small group setting.

The process involves questions or suggestions and silence for reflection after each. Have paper and pens available. Participants jot down notes and phrases at each step. Do not rush through the silences.

- Think for a few moments about why you think it might be helpful for you to have a set of affirmations. What kinds of voices inside do you especially want to counter? Is it fear? Or the urge to drink? Or some self-destructive tendency you notice in yourself? You will want words and phrases that speak especially to your own narrow places. It helps to reflect first on where you struggle.
- Though some prefer simply to string together Bible verses or statements of faith, others will find it helpful to use a framework for their reflections. Have participants try to articulate an affirmation using the

form "Blessed am I when. . . ." (e.g., "Blessed am I when I am able to speak my anger directly" or "Blessed am I when I make time each day to breathe deeply and listen for God").

- Affirmations are sometimes called *personal* affirmations because they reflect the experience of the person who will use them. A compulsive gambler, for instance, might make reference both to gambling and to using his family's rent money to do it. One of his affirmations might read like this: "Blessed am I when I care for my family by using my paycheck for rent and food." One of his lamentations might read, "Woe to me when I believe I can control myself once I've walked into a casino." Then might follow a word from Scripture or a song that speaks God's offer of healing: for example, "I will make a way in the wilderness, says the LORD" (Isa. 43:19) or "I will do a new thing in you." What experience would you like to name? How might you frame that experience as an affirmation? A lamentation?
- Which parts of Christian faith already speak to your heart? What phrases of songs or Scripture come to you? Which parts of your church's worship are most meaningful to you? Write down what comes to you.
- Do you have a Scripture verse that reminds you who God is? Or who you are to God?
- What carries you through difficult times now? What has carried you in the past?

If affirmations are developed in the context of recovery, the leader may also include these questions:

- What kind of support do you want for this next step of your recovery?
- How might affirmations help you from falling into "stinking thinking" or into behaviors you want to leave behind?
- Review with participants the section of chapter 5 that explores lamentations. Then consider this: Are there ways that you might find it helpful to express lamentations as part of your affirmations? Here's an example: At step 7 of the 12 steps, "Humbly asked Him to remove our shortcomings," as part of turning over character defects, someone in recovery might use a lamentation to say, "Woe is me when I expect perfection in myself or in others." An affirmation might be paired with it: "Blessed am I when I am gentle with my own or others' shortcomings, affirming that God alone is perfect."

There is a second, deeper level to the preparation of affirmations. This part will only work when leader and participant know each other well, where trust has already been developed, or when the small group in which the affirmations are being prepared is already well established. This phase might take place in a second session, perhaps a week later.

The leader or group members take time to offer reflections of a person's strengths to him or her (e.g., "I appreciate your ability to listen to others" or "I'm always struck by how creative you are in problem solving"). They may also offer a biblical verse that seems appropriate for the person, or find a way to speak the faith for that person (e.g., "You are a child of God" or "Be still, and know that I am God!" [Ps. 46:10]).

Many addicts find affirmations like these impossible to believe: "I am a child of God"; "I am a sexual being"; "I am loved unconditionally." When there is trust, it is sometimes possible for the leader or group participants to name things in the other person that he or she cannot see—a person's strengths, for example, or his or her value to their community—and in speaking them aloud may be able to offer them as a gift to the other. Reflected in the other's eyes, an addict may be surprised by grace or may learn that others see God differently, less harshly than she has. Voicing her personal affirmations in the context of a relationship with someone willing and able to see her strengths and her failings can help her to live into the future, to act as if the affirmations were true, even when they don't feel true. Affirmations used in this way can become a bridge into further steps in recovery.

FORMING THE AFFIRMATIONS

Participants may work on the next phase of preparation on their own.

Have participants look over the material they have gathered together from answering the questions. Even if in a group setting, each member of the group can read through the material at the same time, quietly, but aloud. Speaking the phrases out loud will help to sort, eliminate, and arrange the material. Awkward phrases will become apparent and may be dropped. Many people discover that personal affirmations work best when they can be committed to memory. Reading the parts aloud will illustrate the phrases can be easily committed to memory.

Participants may also find it helpful to read their affirmations aloud to another person or to have someone read aloud along with them.

Some affirmations are quite long, and some people are able to memorize long sections of text. Even so, it may be useful to choose a section of the affirmation that is especially important, a phrase that can stand in for the whole longer set of affirmations to use when there is not time for the whole. Have participants review the set of affirmations. Are there phrases more crucial than others? Are there sections of text that work especially well, like a prayer, that when spoken slowly, with deep breathing, can bring the one who uses them to a place of calm? What words and phrases come back effortlessly? These are the heart of the affirmations, a part that can stand in for the whole.

FOR FURTHER READING

George Appleton, editor. *The Oxford Book of Prayer*. Oxford: Oxford University Press, 1985.

Gabe Huck. *How Can I Keep from Singing? Thoughts about Liturgy for Musicians*. Archdiocese of Chicago: Liturgy Training Publications, 1989.

William B. McClain. *Come Sunday: The Liturgy of Zion. A Companion to Songs of Zion*. Nashville: Abingdon Press, 1981.

Alice Parker. *The Reasons Why We Sing—Community Song with Alice Parker*. Videotape and Leader's Guide. Archdiocese of Chicago: Liturgy Training Publications, 1995. www.aliceparker.com

Desmond Tutu. *An African Prayer Book*. New York: Doubleday, 1995.

Edward P. Wimberly. *Using Scripture in Pastoral Counseling*. Nashville: Abingdon Press, 1994.

Acknowledgments

With this volume, the publisher Westminster John Knox Press grants permission for readers to duplicate any of the worship materials provided here for their use in a local congregation or ministry setting. For your use in your ministry, you may print, copy, or adapt *any of the rituals* in this book without securing further copyright permission as long as a credit line is listed on every printed copy that includes the following: "[Name of piece] by [name of author and/or composer], © [name of copyright holder], as found in Janet S. Peterman, *Speaking to Silence: New Rites for Christian Worship and Healing* (Louisville, KY: Westminster John Knox Press, 2007). Used by permission."

Grateful acknowledgment is given to the publishers and authors of the following works for the use of copyrighted text:

George Appleton, *Jerusalem Prayers for the World Today* (London: SPCK, 1974). Used by permission of SPCK.

John Bell, "A Cradling Song," copyright © 1996, Wild Goose Resource Group, Iona Community, Scotland. GIA Publications, Inc., exclusive North American agent, 7404 S. Mason Ave., Chicago, IL 60638. www.giamusic.com. 800.442.1358. All rights reserved. Used by permission.

Thomas O. Chisholm, "Great Is Thy Faithfulness." © 1923. Renewal 1951 Hope Publishing Co., Carol Stream, IL 60188. All rights reserved. Used by permission.

Susan Cole, "A Ritual of Cleansing and Renewal Following an Abortion," in *Wisdom's Feast: Sophia in Study and Celebration*, New ed. by Susan Cole, Marian Ronan, and Hal Taussig (Kansas City, MO: Sheed & Ward, 1996). Used with permission.

Florence Gelo, "Caring for the Bereaved Survivors of Suicide," © 2004 by Florence Gelo. 1505 Firethorne Lane, Wyndmoor, PA 19038. Used with permission.

Fred Pratt Green, "O Christ, the Healer We Have Come" © 1969. Hope Publishing Co., Carol Stream, IL 60188. All rights reserved. Used by permission.

Judy Hart, *Love, Judy: Letters of Hope and Healing for Women with Breast Cancer* (Berkeley, CA: Conari Press, 1993). Used with permission.

Marty Haugen, "Shepherd Me, O God," *Shepherd Me, O God* (Chicago: GIA Publications, Inc., 1987). Used with permission.

Muus Jacobse, "We Who Once Were Dead," © 1967 Gooi en Stricht, BV., Baarn, The Netherlands. All rights reserved. Exclusive agent for English-language countries: OCP Publications, 5536 NE Hassalo, Portland, OR 97213. Used with permission.

Dr. Martin Luther King Jr., "Letter from Birmingham City Jail," in *A Testament of Hope: The Essential Writings of Martin Luther King Jr.*, ed. James Melvin Washington. Reprinted by arrangement with the Estate of Martin Luther King, Jr., c/o Writers House as agent for the proprietor, New York, NY. Copyright © 1963 Martin Luther King, Jr., copyright renewed 1991 Coretta Scott King. Used with permission.

Elana Klugman, "Without," in *The New Our Bodies, Ourselves* (New York: Simon & Schuster, 1992). Used with permission.

Violet Cucciniello Little, unpublished sermon, St. Michael's Lutheran Church, Philadelphia, PA, July 22, 2001. Used with permission.

Audre Lourd, "The Transformation of Silence into Language and Action." Reprinted with permission from *Sister Outsider: Essays and Speeches* by Audre Lourd. Copyright © 1984 by Audre Lourd, Ten Speed Press, Berkeley, CA. www.tenspeed.com.

Trapeta B. Mayson, "Healing Song," © 2003 Trapeta B. Mayson; extracts from "I Long to Be," © 1997 Trapeta B. Mayson; and "For Some Sisters," © 1997 Trapeta B. Mayson. Trapeta@aol.com. Used with permission.

Sharon McClain-Boyer, "Grief Support Gathering for Survivors of Homicide" © 1993 Sharon McClain-Boyer. SharonWillie@aol.com. Used with permission.

Roy Oswald, "Personal Affirmation" (unpublished paper). 5658 Amos Reeder Road, Boonsboro, MD 21713. Used with permission.

Janet S. Peterman, "Remembrance and Commendation: A Rite to Speak to Losses in Pregnancy," was first published in *Lutheran Partners* (July/August 1988): 21–24.

Janet S. Peterman and Kathleen Hoye Powell, "A Fellowship Meal with the Family of a Chronically Ill or Disabled Child" © 2001. Used with permission.

"Proper Preface for Christmas," from *Lutheran Book of Worship Ministers'*

Desk Edition © 1978 by permission of Augsburg Fortress. Used with permission.

Rabbi Jack Riemer and Rabbi Sylvan Kamens, "We Remember Them," © 1970. JackRiemer@aol.com. Used with permission.

Carl Sandburg, "Stars, Songs, Faces" from *Smoke and Steel* by Carl Sandburg, copyright © 1920 by Harcourt, Inc. and renewed 1948 by Carl Sandburg, reprinted by permission of the publisher.

May Sarton, "Of Grief" from *Collected Poems 1930–1993* by May Sarton. Copyright © 1993, 1988, 1984, 1980, 1974 by May Sarton. Used by permission of W. W. Norton & Company, Inc., and A.M. Heath and Company.

Marguerite H. Sexton, "Reclaiming a Place of Violence." Copyright © by Marguerite H. Sexton 1993 Journeys of the Heart, 547 Gibson Ave., Jenkintown, PA 19046. Used with permission.

Frederic Shaffmaster, prayer, October 11, 2001. Used with permission.

Jan Struther, "Lord of All Hopefulness." Text: Jan Struther [Joyce Placzek, née Torrens] (1901–1953) © Oxford University Press 1931. Used by permission. All rights reserved. Photocopying this copyright material is ILLEGAL.

Iyanla Vanzant, "Prayer for Spiritual Strength," in *Tapping the Power Within: A Path of Self-Empowerment for Black Women* (New York: Harlem River Press, 1992). Used with permission.

Nicholas Wolterstorff, *Lament for a Son* (Grand Rapids: Wm. B. Eerdmans Publishing Co., 1987). Used with permission from Wm. B. Eerdmans Publishing Co. and SPCK.

John C. Ylvisaker, "I Was There to Hear Your Borning Cry," verse 4, Text and Tune: Copyright © 1985, John C. Ylvisaker, Box 321, Waverly, IA 50677. (319) 352-4396. Used with permission.

Notes

INTRODUCTION

1. Tom F. Driver, *Liberating Rites: Understanding the Transformative Power of Ritual* (Boulder, CO: Westview Press, 1998), 96. Originally published as *The Magic of Ritual: Our Need for Liberating Rites that Transform Our Lives and Our Communities* (San Francisco: Harper, 1991), 96.

2. *Lutheran Book of Worship: Ministers Desk Edition* (Minneapolis: Augsburg, 1978), 246. The text cited is part of the Proper Preface for Christmas.

CHAPTER ONE: HOW CAN I KEEP FROM SINGING?

1. Marty Haugen, "Shepherd Me, O God," *Shepherd Me, O God* (Chicago: GIA Publications, Inc., 1987), 13–14.

2. The echoes of Bela Chagall's description of the arrival of the Sabbath (Shabbos) may be heard here. Cited and explicated by Gabe Huck in *How Can I Keep from Singing: Thoughts about Liturgy for Musicians* (Chicago: Liturgy Training Publications, 1989), 18–23.

3. From "Silence" in *Assembly* 9, no. 1 (September 1982): 184.

4. Elaine Ramshaw, *Ritual and Pastoral Care* (Philadelphia: Fortress Press, 1987), 29.

5. Tom F. Driver, *Liberating Rites: Understanding the Transformative Power of Ritual* (Boulder, CO: Westview Press, 1998), 52, 75.

6. The first line and common title of a gospel song by F. C. Barnes.

7. Ramshaw, *Ritual and Pastoral Care,* 31–32.

CHAPTER TWO: LISTENING FOR GOD'S WORD

1. Victor Witter Turner, *The Forest of Symbols* (Ithaca, NY: Cornell University Press, 1967), 19. See Turner's whole discussion of one symbol in a ritual and its shades of meaning on pp. 19–25.

2. Elaine Ramshaw, *Ritual and Pastoral Care* (Philadelphia: Fortress Press, 1987), 29.

3. Nicholas Wolterstorff, *Lament for a Son* (Grand Rapids: Wm. B. Eerdmans Publishing Co., 1987), 38, 40, 41.

4. Dietrich Bonhoeffer, *Life Together* (New York: Harper & Row, 1954), 59.

5. Ramshaw, *Ritual and Pastoral Care*, 19.

6. Elie Wiesel, *The Oath* (New York: Avon Books, 1973), 224.

CHAPTER THREE: RITUAL SIGNS OF NEW LIFE AND NEW COMMUNITY

1. From an article about Lior Liebling's bar mitzvah: "A Community Basks in His Light," *The Philadelphia Inquirer,* May 24, 2004, B1.

2. Rachel Naomi Remen, "Making Caring Visible," in *Kitchen Table Wisdom: Stories That Heal* (New York: Riverhead Books, 1996), 151–53.

3. John Ylvisaker, "I Was There to Hear Your Borning Cry," in *Songs of the People* (Waverly, IA: New Generation Publishers, 1985), 29.

4. The idea of blessing circles is mine and new to this context. But to Ronald Grimes I am indebted for the notion of a wedding enacting, creating a wedded couple, and to the idea of an active blessing of families and friends as part of that enactment. See his *Marrying and Burying: Rites of Passage in a Man's Life* (San Francisco: Westview Press, 1995), especially chap. 7, "A Wedding that Weds," 84–102.

5. Terry Steele and David Elliott, "Here and Now," © 1989 Universal–MCA Music Publishing, A Division of Universal Studios Inc., D.L.E. Music, and Steele Nickel Music.

6. Jan Struther, "Lord of All Hopefulness," *Lutheran Book of Worship* (New York: Oxford University Press, 1931), 469.

7. This text of the Apostles' Creed was prepared by the International Consultation on English Texts (ICET). It is amended here for inclusive language.

8. From a contribution by Joel Mog in "Readers Write: Names," *The Sun: A Magazine of Ideas* 262 (October 1997): 32–33.

CHAPTER FOUR: MAKING HOLY WHAT HAS BEEN VIOLATED

1. Martin Luther King Jr., "Letter from Birmingham City Jail," in *A Testament of Hope: The Essential Writings of Martin Luther King, Jr.,* ed. James Melvin Washington (San Francisco: Harper and Row, Publishers, 1986), 290.

2. Edward P. Wimberly, *African American Pastoral Care* (Nashville: Abingdon Press, 1991), 39.

3. May Sarton's "Of Grief" in *Collected Poems 1930–1973* (New York: W. W. Norton, 1974), 395.

4. Carl Sandburg, "Stars, Songs, Faces" in *Smoke and Steel* (New York: Harcourt, Brace and Company, 1920), 123.

5. Rabbis Jack Riemer and Sylvan Kamens, "We Remember Them." First published as "At the Rising of the Sun," in *New Prayers for the High Holy Days,* ed. Rabbi Jack Riemer (Bridgeport, CT: The Prayer Book Press of Media Judaica Inc., 1970).

6. Linda Hogan, "department of the interior" in *minding the body: women writers on body and soul,* ed. Patricia Foster (New York: Doubleday, 1994), 173.

7. These Zulu words mean the same thing as the English words found in the previous two lines.

8. *Lutheran Book of Worship* (Minneapolis: Augsburg, 1978), 102.

CHAPTER FIVE: RITUALS FOR RECOVERY

1. Listed in the version used in Alcoholics Anonymous (AA), the twelve steps are:

1. We admitted we were powerless over alcohol—that our lives had become unmanageable. 2. Came to believe that a Power greater than ourselves could restore us to sanity. 3. Made a decision to turn our will and our lives over to the care of God *as we understood Him*. 4. Made a searching and fearless moral inventory of ourselves. 5. Admitted to God, to ourselves, and to another human being the exact nature of our wrongs. 6. Were entirely ready to have God remove all these defects of character. 7. Humbly asked Him to remove our shortcomings. 8. Made a list of all persons we had harmed, and became willing to make amends to them all. 9. Made direct amends to such people wherever possible, except when to do so would injure them or others. 10. Continued to take personal inventory and when we were wrong promptly admitted it. 11. Sought through prayer and meditation to improve our conscious contact with God *as we understood Him*, praying only for knowledge of His will for us and the power to carry that out. 12. Having had a spiritual awakening as the result of these steps, we tried to carry this message to alcoholics, and to practice these principles in all our affairs (*Twelve Steps and Twelve Traditions*, 5–9).

2. Personal correspondence, October 21, 2002.

3. George Appleton, *Jerusalem Prayers for the World Today* (London: SPCK, 1974).

4. Ian Frazier, "On the Rez: Modern Tales of Ordinary Life and Extraordinary Valor in the Hard Land of the Oglala Sioux," *Atlantic Monthly*, December 1999, 81.

5. Ibid., 82.

6. Frederic Shaffmaster, prayer, October 11, 2001.

7. Roy M. Oswald, "Personal Affirmation" (unpublished paper).

8. Margaret Bullitt-Jonas, *Holy Hunger: A Woman's Journey from Food Addiction to Spiritual Fulfillment* (New York: Vintage Books, 2000), 105.

9. Ruben Schindler, "The Halakhic Framework of Mourning and Bereavement: Its Implications in Dealing with Crisis," *Tradition: A Journal of Orthodox Thought* 15, no. 3 (1975): 69–80. The quotation may be found on pages 70–71.

10. Caroline Knapp, *Drinking: A Love Story* (New York: Dell Publishing, 1996), 278–79.

11. Thomas O. Chisholm, "Great is Thy Faithfulness," *The New National Baptist Hymnal* (Nashville: Triad Publications, 1977), 153. © 1923. Renewal 1951 Hope Publishing Co., Carol Stream, IL 60188. All rights reserved. Used by permission.

12. See, for example, studies cited in Judith A. Lewis, ed., *Addictions: Concepts and Strategies for Treatment* (Gaithersburg, MD: Aspen Publishers, Inc., 1994), 8–9.

13. Knapp, *Drinking: A Love Story*, 268–69.

14. Violet Cucciniello Little (sermon, St. Michael's Lutheran Church, Philadelphia, PA, July 22, 2001).

15. Iyanla Vanzant, "Prayer for Spiritual Strength," in *Tapping the Power Within: A Path of Self-Empowerment for Black Women* (New York: Harlem River Press, 1992), 110.

CHAPTER SIX: RITUALS OF BLESSING IN THE PRESENCE OF DEATH

1. Alexander McCall Smith, *The No. 1 Ladies' Detective Agency* (Edinburgh: Polygon, 1998), 100.

2. Psalm 139 is reprinted from *Book of Common Prayer* (New York: Church Hymnal Corp., 1979).

3. Kim Kluger-Bell, *Unspeakable Losses: Understanding the Experience of Pregnancy Loss, Miscarriage, and Abortion* (New York: W. W. Norton & Company, Inc., 1998), 96.

4. Fred Pratt Green, "O Christ, the Healer," *Lutheran Book of Worship* (New York: Oxford University Press, 1931), 360. © 1969. Hope Publishing Co., Carol Stream, IL 60187. All rights reserved. Used by permission.

5. Steve Austin and Cathy Hitchcock, *Breast Cancer: What You Should Know (But May Not Be Told) about Prevention, Diagnosis, and Treatment* (Rocklin, CA: Prima Publishing, 1994), 57.

6. Edward Hopper, "Jesus, Savior, Pilot Me," *Lutheran Book of Worship,* # 334.

7. Judy Hart, *Love, Judy: Letters of Hope and Healing for Women with Breast Cancer* (Berkeley, CA: Conari, 1993), 34.

8. Ibid., 25–28. Italics mine.

9. Elana Klugman, "Without" in *The New Our Bodies, Ourselves* (New York: Simon & Schuster, 1992).

10. Hart, *Letters of Hope*, 36.

11. John Ellerton, 1826–93. Verse 1 of "Savior Again to Thy Dear Name We Raise." *Service Book and Hymnal* (Minneapolis: Augsburg Publishing House, 1958), 198.

12. In the early church, Christians would carry the body of the deceased to the place of burial, singing psalms and hymns as they traveled. As Thomas G. Long notes, "The dead were seen as saints traveling on to God. . . . The journey to the cemetery carrying the body of the deceased . . . was, for early Christians, not just part of the funeral. It *was* the funeral." "O Sing to Me of Heaven: Preaching at Funerals" by Thomas G. Long, *Journal for Preachers* 29, no. 3 (2006): 23.

13. From the CD *Donnie McClurkin*. Warner Alliance of Warner Bros. Records, Inc. 1996. Track 1.

14. Ibid.

15. From the CD *Wow Gospel 2004*. Disc 1. Track 11.

16. From the CD *Closer: Josh Groban*. 2003. Track 12.

CHAPTER SEVEN: CREATING NEW WORSHIP MATERIALS

1. Ps. 139:15 is reprinted from *Book of Common Prayer* (1979).

2. David O'Reilly, "Mennonites Expel Church for Taking Gay Members," *Philadelphia Inquirer*, October 17, 1997, B1.

3. From "Symbol" by V. H. Kooy in the *Interpreter's Dictionary of the Bible*, ed. George Arthur Buttrick (Nashville: Abingdon Press, 1962), 4:472.

4. Nicholas Wolterstorff, *Lament for a Son* (Grand Rapids: Wm. B. Eerdmans Publishing Co., 1987), 40–41.

5. Roy M. Oswald, "Personal Affirmation" (unpublished paper).

Contributors

Susan Cole is a United Methodist pastor whose primary ministry is spiritual direction. She has served four congregations, all in the city of Philadelphia.

Florence Gelo is a Unitarian Universalist minister and pastoral psychotherapist in private practice specializing in chronic illness, grief, and loss.

Sharon McClain-Boyer lost her youngest son, Kevin Lamont, to homicide in 1990. She served as the victims' representative for twelve years on the Ohio Criminal Sentencing Commission, a commission responsible for revising felony, misdemeanor, and juvenile laws for the State of Ohio.

Trapeta B. Mayson, born in Liberia, is a poet living and working in Philadelphia. Artist in Residence at Art Sanctuary in North Philadelphia and host of various neighborhood poetry readings, she has won fellowships from the Pew Foundation and the Pennsylvania Council on the Arts.

Kathleen Hoye Powell is a social worker who teaches at Frostburg State University in Maryland. She lives with her husband, Fred, and their daughter, Abby, in the mountains of western Maryland. Their son, Joshua, died early in 2006.

Marguerite Sexton credits her Roman Catholic upbringing with her love of ritual. Since creating "Reclaiming a Place of Violence," she has crafted many rituals, usually for people who are not affiliated with traditional religious organizations or for situations in which traditional religious organizations do not minister.